Observations

The Hard Truths

WARNING:

Some topics contained in this book are not politically correct and may upset you. Read this book at your own risk. The publisher and author may not be held responsible for any emotional, financial or any other type of damages resulting from you reading this book.

Written by Donal Shunney

Observations

The Hard truths

by

Donal Shunney

Published 2010

Printed in the United States of America

Copyright@ 2009

Library of Congress

Cataloging in Publication Data

Shunney, Donald

Observations

I.   Observations The Hard Truths

13 Digit ISBN Trade 978-1-449-56608-1
10 Digit ISBN Trade 1-4495-6608-1

Published November 2009

1st Printing

Warning

Some topics contained in this book are not politically correct and may upset you. Read this book at your own risk. The publisher and author may not be held responsible for any emotional, financial or any other type of damages resulting from you reading this book.

Disclaimer

The author and publishing company shall have neither liability nor responsibility to any person or entity with respect to any loss or damages arising from the information contained in this book.

The opinions expressed in this book belong to the author.

Trademark Acknowledgements

All terms mentioned in this book that are known to be trademarks or service marks have been appropriately capitalized. Use of a term should not be regarded as affecting the validity of any trademark or service mark.

About the Author

Donal Shunney lived in New England before moving to Michigan in 2002. He is currently enrolled in Henry Ford Community College to obtain a degree in information assurance.

Dedication

I would like to dedicate this book to all the people who lack common sense and intelligence. By no means am I implying I am a genius but come on, without you this book would not have been possible. Now think about it, are you the person who thinks "What dumbass did that" or are you the person who thinks "I am a dumbass for doing that". For those who think "I am a dumbass for doing that" or something similar, I would like to thank you and let you know, keep up the good work. I would like to write Observations: The Hard truths part II.

I told you this book was not going to be politically correct so if you're offended, oh well. I warned you.

Acknowledgements

Dr. Gregory

Thank you. You are one of the best doctors I have ever had. Without your help I do not think I would be alive today. You have helped me see that people do care and can change things.

Dr. Neumann

Thank you. You helped me see things differently when we talked about the topics contained in this book. Without your help I never would have written this book.

Kelly Meehhean

Thank you for the support you showed me when writing this book and for believing in me.

Lori Knight

Thank you for proof reading this book, the support, the suggestions and the ideas for new topics. I love you.

Tara Z.

Thank you for all the help you provided with getting this book published

Tarick Carver

Thank you for the assistance with the driving study and playing the devil's advocate when it came to talking about the topics of this book

Teri Palmer

Thank you for discussing some of the topics in the book with me and helping me see a different side to them.

Zeitgeist

While I did not use any of the statistics from the movie Zeitgeist since I am unable to contact them for permission, I feel I need to thank them anyways for making that movie. The movie helped provide me with insights on topics I never would have researched. The information in this movie was unbelievable.

John and Faye

Thank you for assisting with the editing of this book. I appreciate the help very much.

My friends who are not mentioned

I spent my days researching the topics and discussing the topics with many of you. It must have seemed like this was all I could talk about. I am pretty sure I annoyed a few of you. Without your support I am not sure if this book would have ever been written. I want all of you who discussed the topics of this book with me to know how much I truly appreciate it.

Contents

Things you can change about yourself

Not politically correct

Things you can change about society

Contents

My thoughts

Prelude

Many people seem to accept whatever happens until it is inconvenient or causes them harm, even if they disagree with it. The only time people band together in America is when something tragic happens. Then after a while they lose interest and just go back to their lives.

A great example of this would be the airports. People want to make sure the plane won't be hijacked, but yet bitch about the longer lines. Do people really think measures to protect them can be put into effect without sacrificing something in return?

I am not out to please you with this book so don't read it with that in mind. The intention of this book is to wake you up and possibly knock sense into others. I hope it will make you question things enough to actually help try and change them.

If you get to the end of this book and think nothing is wrong or believe nothing needs to change then you really need to wake the hell up. I don't expect you to agree with every idea in this book. The ideas in the book are not a fix-all; they are just ideas to get you to think about alternative solutions.

If you agree with parts of this book then you need to do something about it. You may not agree with my solutions but if you agree with what is wrong, get off your ass and do something about it. I am writing this book to help start the process.

The questions I am hoping it will make you ask are:

- *Why have I allowed these things to happen?*
- *Why haven't I done something sooner?*
- *How can I find this acceptable?*
- *How can I help things change?*

I am the type of person who pays attention to the little things. When things don't work or make sense I have no problem with asking questions. I have no problem voicing my opinion or speaking my mind about things. I am not concerned with what you think about my opinions and I am not saying I am right. I can admit when I am wrong. Can you?

While the truth can hurt sometimes, it doesn't mean it should go unsaid. The truth hurts less than a lie.

You should be willing to accept the reality of life and you can't expect someone to shelter you from the pains of life. If you think sheltering someone from life's lessons is a good thing then you need a reality check.

If you have a child that you protect from all pain and hardships in life then what is going to happen when you are not there to protect them?

I believe certain things are instilled in you at a young age. I have always tried to believe that common sense and a basic intelligence are just two of them. I have learned over the years that some people have no common sense and every time I think the human race cannot get any dumber, someone always comes along and proves me wrong.

Many people do things that don't make sense or show how little common sense they have. Most things in life require common sense and not a degree.

There is a difference between what society was like 20 years ago and what it has become. I know as time passes things will change. I believe some of the changes have made society a better place, but some have not. There are things in society that I don't believe work and need to be fixed. I hear people bitch about many of the same concerns I have but they do nothing about them. Has society become so complacent that people don't really care? Would you rather just accept what is wrong and complain about it instead trying to fix it?

Life has no owner's manual or warning labels attached. All you can do is live by the values instilled in you by your parents and instill even better values in your children. Hopefully this will make the world a better place for the next generation.

You chose to read this book, for better or worse and it should make you think about things. You may choose to do nothing or choose to do something with the topics you agree with. However, the choice can only be made by you. If you chose to do nothing you can only blame yourself.

Unless things change, society will keep going down the same path. You cannot expect someone else to change what you don't like and keep what you like.

If you want things to change, the best place to start is with your child. If you don't start with them, then what is the point? The children are our future and unless you help them develop better values, the world is pretty much screwed. There seems to be less and less to offer our children. I have heard people say "Chivalry is dead". Is it really dead or just lost on most people? If you think it is dead, then do something to bring it back. Chivalry can be brought back, it all starts with you. It all has to do with family values. When your child has family values, they will do right by you and the world.

Things you can change about yourself

Family Values

Your child learns in different ways. One way is called a "learned behavior." A "learned behavior" is a behavior that is observed.

Some of the things the children of today need to learn are family values. Family values are a very important part of society. As an adult you should not expect your child to learn them from anyone else but you. If you do not instill family values into your child, who will? They will not learn them from school, friends, TV, radio or the Internet. Your child will learn from your actions or inactions.

Family values need to be taught to children at a young age. They are more than just words; they are a belief and a lifestyle. When you fail to teach your child manners, respect, honesty, responsibility, discipline, morals, integrity, honor and family values you fail yourself, them and society. Teaching family values to a child is not hard and learning them is not hard. The hard part is living by them and that needs to start with you. You are the one who decides how you act in society.

*Teach your child **manners** and they will learn respect. Teach your child **respect** and they will learn honesty. Teach your child **honesty** and they will learn responsibility. Teach your child **responsibility** and they will learn morals. Teach your child **morals** and they will learn discipline. Teach your child **discipline** and they will learn integrity. Teach your child **integrity** and they will learn honor. Teach your child **honor** and they will develop good character. When your child has all of these, they will learn **family values**.*

Just because your child learns what these are does not, by any means, mean they will demonstrate them. As the parent it is up to you to show your child that these are important in life and are more than words.

The best way to teach a child something is by demonstration and not just telling them.

You can tell your child to do as you say and not as you do, but what kind of example are you really setting? Do you really think that child is going to do as you say or as you act? You are the role model... Aren't you?

The best place to start all this is with manners. Use them whenever you're interacting with anyone even if your child is not around. If you use them when your child isn't with you, then they will become a habit so you will use them when they are.

Manners are the rules of social conduct, which show the person to be cultured, polite, and refined.

You are the one who is responsible for teaching your child manners. You cannot expect your child to use them if you don't use them. Children do not learn just from what you tell them, they learn from your actions. You cannot expect a child to forget something or ignore something you do. The way a child acts is usually a direct reflection on you.

If you use manners when interacting with others your child will learn them. If you don't use them, your child won't either. So who is to blame? You are the only one to blame. Your child may learn them in time, but do you want them taught to your child by someone else?

I was in a store one day and I was behind a mother who had her daughter with her. She was talking to the cashier and never used manners. She asked the cashier questions and told the cashier to double bag her items. A few seconds later her daughter asked if she could have a candy bar. The mother looks at her daughter and told her to ask nicely. I looked at the cashier and she looked at me and we both could not believe it. I asked the mother how she could expect her daughter to use manners when she doesn't. She gave me a dirty look and never replied. After she left, the cashier and I laughed over how I pretty much shut her up. I actually hope the lady reads the book. She apparently needs to learn something.

How can you expect your child to do something if you're not willing to do it yourself?

It only takes a second to add a "thank you", "please" or "no thank you" to your sentences. People also tend to respond better when manners are used. I personally know when someone is polite to me I will do more for him or her than I do when they are rude or impolite.

I have dealt with all kinds of people in my life and I have always used manners when appropriate. I showed them respect and it was always reciprocated.

When you use manners you are showing a form of respect.

Respect is an act of thoughtfulness or sympathetic regard.

Respect has different meaning for people. On a practical level it includes taking someone's feelings, needs, thoughts, ideas, wishes, beliefs and preferences into consideration. You could say it means taking all of these seriously and giving them worth and value.

When you respect someone, you show him or her they have value with you and you value their thoughts, beliefs, feelings, etc. Using manners when you speak to someone, no matter who they are, shows them you're polite and respectful. This is not the only way to show respect.

Respect is listening to what someone says, holding a door open and helping someone up are just a few of the ways, but not the only ways. There are no set rules on what the proper signs of respect really are. The best guideline I can think of is: *If you want it done to you, do it for others; if you don't want it done to you, don't do it to others.*

Respect cannot be bought, stolen, traded, found or given out of fear. When respect is shown to you as a result of fear, it is not really respect. If you think it is, then you're fooling yourself. If you want real respect, earn it by your actions and the way you treat people. If you want people to treat you with respect then you need to treat them with it.

When you have respect for someone, you should be honest with them.

Honesty *is fairness and straight forwardness of conduct.*

I know there are times when lying can be used on occasion and is beneficial in cases of National Security. The truth may hurt but does it hurt more than a lie? Usually, when you lie to someone you care about; you're doing it to protect them. Is it really protecting them? They will find out the truth sooner or later. Then they will feel the hurt from the lie and might find it hard to trust you.

There are different types of lies, some of which are fabrication, bold-faced, by omission, to-children, white, noble, emergency, perjury, bluffing, misleading and let's not leave out the promotional lie. Shouldn't a lie be a lie? Whatever happened to the old saying "Honesty is the best policy?"

In order to be honest with others, you should be honest with yourself and be willing to handle the truth. If you can't be truthful with yourself, how can you really be truthful with anyone else?

Your friend is wearing an outfit that looks really bad and they ask you what you think. Would you be honest (in a polite way) or lie to them? Think about it for a minute before reading on.

Now, if you would lie to them, what if you were wearing it? Would you want them to be honest or lie to you?

When you're honest, you should take responsibility for your actions and inactions.

Responsibility is a moral, legal, or mental accountability.

Responsibility is something you need to take. Blaming someone else for your problems or something that happens is always easier, but how can you expect your children to be responsible if you aren't? No one else is responsible for the actions you take, but you.

Taking responsibility is a very important part of society. You need to take responsibility, not only for your actions, but your inactions as well. When you take responsibility it shows you are willing to accept the consequences, good or bad. You will make mistakes. Everyone does; it's called the human factor. It is one of the ways we learn.

If you teach your child someone else is always responsible for anything bad that happens, eventually no one will take responsibility.

When you use something, as it's not intended, it isn't the company's fault. You used it wrong so step up and take responsibility.

As a child, if I played with a toy wrong and got hurt. It was not the manufacturer's fault; it was mine. I heard many times "that will teach you to play with it the right away" and it did.

Today, when something bad happens as a result of you doing something wrong, you can sue the company for not informing you of what could go wrong. Whatever happened to common sense? Coffee cups have to have warning labels on them because the contents may be hot. No way, "hot coffee" that is hot? You have to be kidding me. If you asked for coffee and it was not hot, you would bring it back and complain. You know it.

When you're responsible, it demonstrates to others that you have morals.

Morals *are a code of conduct in matters concerning right and wrong. Morals are created and defined by individual conscience, society and religion.*

When you have morals, you would do something despite what others think because you know it would be the right thing to do. Morals are hard to find in people today. Most people will do anything for money.

Morals are not that complicated to instill into your child. If you have them and live by them, then your child will have a better chance of living by them as well.

Morals can even make it hard for you to find a lasting relationship, since so many people think someone who has morals is too good to be true.

When you have morals, you demonstrate you have discipline.

Discipline *is the ability to restrain your behavior or emotions to remain within societies rules of conduct.*

Being disciplined does not mean you keep your feelings locked up inside you; it means you have the ability to express them in a controlled way. Discipline is important since it helps you act within the rules of society, despite how you feel or what is going on around you.

You do not have to always have your child take a time out or spank them to get them to understand. Granted, different ages and maturity level of the child should be taken into account. Sometimes, though, when a child does something you should take a look at yourself and see if it is something you actually do. You cannot use the old saying, "Do as I say and not as I do," when it comes to children. Set an example for them to follow. If you can't then how can you discipline a child for doing something you do?

When you are disciplined, you demonstrate integrity.

Integrity *is a firm adherence to a code of exceptional morale.*

The word integrity has many uses, but the one I am referring to is a quality of a person's character. Integrity can be described in part as the relationship you have with yourself. It is the way you act and not just when it is convenient, but all the time. It means doing the right thing even when nobody is watching. It is not easy having integrity; it takes a conscious effort on your part. It should be reinforced regularly.

Having integrity is a good thing. It will mean you not only have principles and a code you live by, but you actually follow them and set an example for your children.

When you have integrity, you demonstrate honor.

Honor is a measure of your honesty, respect and integrity.

Honor is defined not only by your words, but your actions as well. Honor is more than just a word though. Honor cannot be stolen, bought or borrowed. It cannot be given to you. It cannot be forced on you. It is a part of you. You either have it or you don't.

You cannot have honor only when it benefits you. In some places a person's worth is determined solely by their honor. Honor is great, it means people can trust you and trust what you say. The one thing to remember is to say what you mean and mean what you say. Never make a promise you can't keep and never break a promise you make.

When you have honor, you will demonstrate good character.

Character is how others see you, your reputation.

The way you act to others is one of the things that determine if you have good or bad character. When you have good character you will see a difference in the way people act or react to you. Your reputation is not always based on your actions, but sometimes it is based on your inaction. Sometimes people will know you before you even know them and this is how they will judge you.

When you know these to be more than just words and you live by these, you will know what family values are.

Family values do vary from family to family and from culture to culture. You are the only one who can instill family values into your child. You need to instill them with your words and actions. Not one or the other. When your child has all of these and lives by them, you should be proud, they learned them from you. You have a child you can be more than just proud of; you will have a child that will make the world a better place.

If you want your children to grow up in a better world, you have to show your child you are willing to help make it better. If you don't help change what is wrong, do you think they will? If it is good enough for you, why would they want to?

You probably think your child has all of these, but are you sure? Take an honest look at yourself, and think if you do. I do not mean with just friends and family, I mean when you're shopping, when you're at the park or out with your friends. If you don't do all of these, all the time, how can you really expect your child to? You are the one they should be learning them from. If you're hoping your child learns them from someone besides you, you're fooling yourself. The children of today are much different than they were in the past. Children of today have less supervision than when you were a child. Maybe it is a result of your busy life style, but are you really that busy?

Children

As a child you learned right from wrong and what is socially accepted. When you did something wrong, you more than likely got punished for it. When you hear about a child doing something wrong today, who should be blamed? The Parents? The school? The Government? The child? Or do you believe they are all responsible?

When you point the blame at everyone except the child who actually did it, what message are you sending the child? You need to teach them that if they do something wrong there will be consequences. If you don't then the next time they do something wrong they will expect the same thing. One of the ways you teach a child is with discipline. When they do something wrong, they should face the consequences. A punishment is not something they are expected to like or enjoy. If punishments were enjoyable then what would be the point of it?

Punishment *is to impose a penalty for a fault, offense, or violation.*

In today's society a major concern is child abuse. There are different types of abuse that affect our lives and while I wish abuse didn't happen, it does. It does not just happen to children but it happens to adults as well. The types of abuse are emotional, physical, sexual, verbal and mental. I lived with abuse as a child in both my parents' house and in foster homes. There is a difference between smacking your child on the butt and child abuse. I don't care what the experts say. I would personally like to know how many of those experts lived with real abuse.

While all forms of abuse are wrong, each person who lives through it is affected differently. I know how abuse can affect a person first hand and it is not something that can easily be forgotten or left in the past. People have told me "just let it go," "forget it" and "you cannot let the past determine your future." In my experience the ones who say these never lived with it or had to deal with it personally. It stays with the person long after it has stopped. Realistically it cannot be forgotten. How many major events in your life have you forgotten?

There is a difference between disciplining a child with a smack on the butt and child abuse.

Abuse is physical maltreatment to treat cruelly or roughly.

I have visited websites telling you how to discipline your child. How to raise your child and how you should not spank your child. During the research for this topic, I came across one website that had a video with children telling you how they do not like being spanked. If you stopped punishing people because they did not like the punishment then shouldn't all the people incarcerated be set free? I am pretty sure they don't like it either.

Now some of the websites I visited did have things that actually made sense and some things that didn't. I do agree with talking to the child and letting them know what they did was wrong and why. I, however, think that compromising with your children when they are acting up is not right. I have seen children acting up in stores, restaurants, and doctor offices just to name a few places. I have seen some parents offer to buy the child something if they behave. This just does not make sense to me. Your child is acting up so you offer to buy them something so they stop acting up? Has anyone thought what this might teach the child? If they want something, act up until you offer to buy them something. What about the long-term effect? If a child learns this what are they going to do when they want a new car or a promotion at work?

The line between discipline and abuse is so unclear, it is sad. It has gotten to the point where a child can say they were hit by the parents and someone notifies Child Protective Services. The children of today know they can claim child abuse even when there is none. When a child can do this and it keeps the parent from disciplining them, who runs the household?

There are many ways to teach your child discipline. I am not going to tell you how to raise your child or how to discipline them. You're their parent not me.

Kids are bringing guns to school, making bombs and beating each other up.

If your child is not taught there are consequences for their actions why would they stop?

Most states have laws preventing children under a certain age from being charged for a crime. Drug dealers use this law to their benefit. They will use your child to sell the drugs so when they are caught they won't have to worry about doing time. Now, who do these laws actually help? I am by no means saying your child should be sent to prison, but some form of punishment needs to happen. The type of punishment should be based on what was done. The punishment should be something to teach your child not to do it again. I know sometimes your child may not fully understand what they did was wrong. One way to find out if they did or not would be to ask one simple question, would they want it done to them? If they say no, then they had a really good idea it was wrong.

Why would you want to teach your child they are not going to be held accountable until they hit a certain age?

These laws don't protect your child; they give them a free pass. I am not saying they should treat them like adults but they need to learn there are consequences for their actions.

When a child does commit a violent crime, people are shocked and outraged. People are quick to point the finger to the parents, the school, music, television or video games and the child's past. This is bullshit. I was abused and had a bad childhood and I am not a criminal. It is a choice and I don't care what the experts say. Stop making excuses and take responsibility.

Why don't you actually put the blame where it belongs? The person who did the crime is responsible. Isn't it time you stop trying to teach the children there are no consequences for their actions? The old saying "do the crime, do the time" comes to mind.

I know it is a parent's instinct to protect their child, but how many times have you heard, "They are a good child." Maybe they are and they made the wrong choice but that's no reason they shouldn't face the consequences.

There are currently about seventy million Americans under the age of 18, or 25% of the total U.S population.

According to the FBI UCR of 2003

8.6% of juveniles arrested were arrested for murder.
15.2% of juveniles arrested were arrested for rape.

23.9% of juveniles arrested were arrested for robbery.

13.3% of juveniles arrested were arrested for aggravated assault.
If those stats bother you, keep reading and see which ones have increased.

According to the FBI UCR of 2006

9.5% of juveniles arrested were arrested for murder.
14.8% of juveniles arrested were arrested for rape.
26.4% of juveniles arrested were arrested for robbery.

13.1% of juveniles arrested were arrested for aggravated assault.

In 2006, there were 14,380,370 people estimated to be arrested in the U.S 20% of them were under the age of 18.

What you learn as a child will stay with you for your entire life. The greatest impact of what you learned can be seen in the relationships you have.

Relationships

Relationship is the association between two or more people.

The various relationships you have during your life will affect you in some way. All relationships require effort on the part of both people. When you meet someone, the way you interact with them depends on your past and what type of relationship you hope to have. As you get to know someone a friendship develops. In my experience there are two types of friendships: fake and real.

While you can hope to find the people who actually want to be real friends, there are those people who only want to be a friend when it is convenient for them or they want something. These are the ones I call "fake" friends.

Fake friends only talk to you when times are good or when they want something from you. They will be the first to call you when they need something, but never be around when you need something. They are the ones who will talk trash about you when you're not there, but will be nice to your face. They will call you when they have nothing really better to do.

Now the friends you really would like to find in life are the "real" ones. Real friends will be there during the good and bad times. They will be the ones who won't care when you mess up. They won't judge you for your past. They will always have your back and will be the ones you can tell anything to and it stays with them. They will be the ones who bust on you when you're there and not behind your back. They will be the ones who will help you but never expect anything in return. Real friends are the ones you want to keep in your life. They are the ones you can trust.

Beyond friendship are the romantic relationships. Romantic relationships start out because you noticed the other person or they noticed you. When you do meet someone and you're attracted to them, despite what people want to believe or say, looks do matter. While the concept of "looks don't matter" is a great thing, most people who say it are full of shit. Have you ever heard someone say, "I have to meet him or her because they look smart?" No. You can't because you don't know them yet. Usually the people who say, "Looks don't matter" may honestly want to believe it, but they are fooling themselves. Looks do matter in some way and you should be honest with yourself and just admit it. I won't go out with someone if I am not physically and mentally attracted to her. You can call me superficial but at least I am honest enough to admit it. If I am physically attracted to a lady, but not intellectually I won't get involved with her. I need both in a relationship. You think I am superficial and looks don't honestly matter, could you fall totally in love with someone you never met face to face, never saw a picture of them and never asked them to describe themselves? If you can't, then in some way, looks do matter to you.

When you find someone you're attracted to it is natural to try and impress him or her. However, some people take it far beyond this. Some may not be truthful about their real job or they may even act totally against their real character. When you start any type of relationship off this way, it is based off lies. What good is a relationship if it is based on lies or deception? You shouldn't have to impress someone by being what you are not. If you think it is OK to do this, then how would you feel if you were the one being lied to?

Lies

Lie: *A type of deception in the form of an untruthful statement with the intention to deceive.*

Now if you admit it's a lie then ask yourself, why would you want to start a relationship based on lies? If you cannot start a relationship based on the truth, is it really worth having?

In this day and age, so many people are afraid of getting hurt by someone it makes it hard to trust. While I am not great at trusting others, I have learned over the years that if you watch what they say and do, in time, inconsistencies will show through. Anyone can speak the words they think you want to hear, but when it comes to living by them, they will fall short if they were lies. When you do meet someone, you can only hope they are being truthful.

I have heard many people say, "I want to find someone nice." If you have said this and then ended a relationship using the reason, "it is too good to be true," then you really need to think about it. If you really wanted someone nice then you wouldn't have ended the relationship. Stop fooling yourself and be honest. How can you say you want someone nice then break it off with him or her for being good?

When you are lucky enough to find someone worth keeping around there are things that shouldn't be done. To start, don't think you can go into a relationship and change something you don't like about that person. When you are involved with someone you should accept him or her for whom and what they are. If you don't like something to the point you feel you need to change it then maybe you should find someone else.

How would you feel if there was something about you someone did not like and they tried to make you change?

If they try to change you, do you really think they are accepting you for who you are?

While sometimes they may want you to change for the better (health) which is a good thing, you should never change for someone else, you should always change for yourself.

When you're in a relationship, if it lasts long enough it usually leads to falling in love.

Love

Love *is attraction based on sexual desire, affection and tenderness felt by lover's warmth and enthusiasm, or devotion.*

First, let's start out with this:

Ladies, if you don't have any self respect then how the hell can you expect a guy to have it for you?

Guys, if you don't show a lady respect then grow the hell up.

When in a relationship you should both be equals. You are no better than they are and they are no better than you. While you both have different skills and might be better at something it still does not make you better than they are. You should be willing to share your knowledge, likes and dislikes with them and they should be willing to share theirs with you. One of the most important parts of a relationship should be communication.

Love should be respected. So many people use the word just to use it. Love is the only emotion that can cause you to feel all the other emotions. When people say "I love you" just to gain something, it demeans the true meaning of it. When you love someone, that person should be important to you. Their feelings, thoughts and beliefs should matter. It is easy to find reasons why a relationship will not work out. The hard part is finding the reasons for it to work.

You are busy in life and have so many things to worry about. It is easy to say, I don't have time for a relationship. In a relationship, you don't need to spend every day together or all the time on the phone, but on the days when you don't have time to see each other, is it really hard to text someone or call just to say Hi. You may not have more than a few minutes but sometimes, that is all it takes. When you love someone though, you can't expect them to stop what they are doing to reply to your text or answer the phone. When you really love them, knowing it made them smile should be enough.

There is one thing though. You shouldn't expect someone to do the little things for you if you're not willing to do them back. A relationship requires effort from both people, not just one. When one person gives all the time and never gets anything back in return, don't be surprised if the relationship doesn't work or they cheat on you. Now, cheating on someone is one of the worst things you can do to them.

Cheating

Cheating *is defined as sexually unfaithful, lying and deception usually for ones self-interest.*

You have heard the reasons people use when they are caught cheating. People cheat for different reasons, but not everyone has cheated on someone. However most of us know someone who has been cheated on. When you cheat on someone you cause the person you say you care about to hurt in so many ways it can't really be described.

There is never a good reason to cheat on someone. Some of the reasons I have heard are, "I was to drunk," "It just happened" and "I didn't mean to." It does not matter what your reason is. There should never be an acceptable reason to cheat on someone you love.

Cheating on your significant other disrespects them and betrays the trust they put in you. When they do learn that you cheated on them, not only are they hurt by the act of you cheating, but they also are hurt because you lied to them about it. Now if they don't break up with you, how can they trust you again? You can say you won't do it again, but you lied to them already so how can they believe you?

"Sorry," will not take away the pain or help them trust you. If people thought about how much it would hurt their significant other maybe less people would do it.

Do you care about the one you are involved with? If you do then why would you want to hurt them? How would you feel if they cheated on you? If you wouldn't want them to cheat on you, then shouldn't you show them that same respect?

Since the Internet is in so many households people wonder if cybersex is or isn't cheating.

Cybersex

Cybersex *is a virtual sex encounter in which two communicate over the Internet and send each other sexually explicit messages. It is fantasy sex where the two describe their actions in written form. It is designed to stimulate sexual feelings. It is a form of role-playing in which they pretend they are having actual sex.*

The tough question is should it really be considered cheating? People's opinion on this varies, the ones who think it is not, usually are the ones who think it is ok because it is just something to pass the time.

When you are in a relationship and you have cybersex with someone should it be considered cheating? Before answering, think about it. Would you tell your significant other you had cybersex with someone else? If you wouldn't tell them you did, why not? Would you want your significant other to have cybersex with someone else? If you wouldn't, then why is it ok for you and not them?

If more people thought about how they would feel if someone did something to them, maybe people would stop hurting each other so much. Is it really that hard to have respect and to treat someone the way you want them to treat you?

In your life you will come across people who will hurt, betray or disrespect you, it is a fact of life. When that happens, it is nice to have someone there for you. When you try to be there for someone you will try to find a way to communicate.

Communication

Communication *is a process by which you assign and convey meaning in an attempt to create shared understanding.*

One of the things you say to someone who you care about that is hurt is

"I know how you feel"

When you are hurt your friends and family want to help you feel better. When you want to be there for someone one thing that shouldn't be said is "I know how you feel." You actually don't know how they feel. Even if you've been through the same thing you still wouldn't know. You feel things differently and what affects you deeply might not bother someone else as much.

While you are able to relate to how they might feel you can never really know how someone else feels. I know how I feel when something happens to me but that does not tell me how you feel. Try saying, "I can relate to how you feel," but only if you actually can. If you have never been through it then you should try saying, "I can image how you must feel," or "I can't even begin to image how you feel." While trying to sympathize with someone is not a bad thing, telling them you know how they feel is really stupid because you don't and won't.

There are many other things you say to people that actually don't make sense.

There are various ways for you to communicate, speaking, tone of voice, body language, and hand gestures are just a few.

When you communicate, people will ask questions. When I was growing up, I was always told, "There is no such thing as a stupid question." That is so not true. There are lots of dumb questions. Some of them are:

"Why would they tell me that?"
This is a really stupid question. Why would you ask someone else why someone else

told you something? There is only one person who actually knows why they told you what they did, the person who told you.

"Are you ok?"

When someone is injured or crying, why would you ask them if they are ok? If they were OK, would they be crying? If they are injured, you just are an idiot. Try asking the question, "What can I do to help?"

When you communicate with someone on the phone, there should be some basic rules applied out of respect. While some you may not be able to control there are some you can. When one happens you cannot control, pull the phone away from you out of respect for yourself and the person you're talking to.

Burping, coughing, sneezing or sniffling; these ones cannot always be controlled but if they happen move the phone away or apologize for them.

Now, the following can be controlled and if these are done, the person you're on the phone with should have the right to hang up on you or smack you upside the head.

Don't eat when you are on the phone with someone.

People don't want to hear the sounds of you chewing your food. If you're that hungry you should wait to make the phone call or don't pick up the phone.

Don't pick up the phone during sex.

This is just disrespectful to the person you're with. If you're that bored during sex, you're doing something wrong.

Don't use the phone in the movie theater.

You are not the only one in the movie theater trying to watch the movie. If you feel you have to take the call then go to the lobby and stop wrecking the movie for the other people who also paid to see it. If you don't want to miss the movie then let your phone go to voicemail and call the person back later. How would you feel if someone who was sitting around you was talking on the phone? You know you would be telling them to "shhh."

The Bathroom.

When you answer the phone the caller asks, "What are you doing?" The reply is generally nothing because you don't want to tell them you're going to the bathroom. If you would not want to tell them then you know it is not right. What could be so important you feel the need to talk to someone when you're in the bathroom? What could not wait five minutes?

Now, if you're one of those people who purposely make a call when you're going to the bathroom, what the hell are you thinking? Have some courtesy and wait until you're done.

If you can't follow some basic etiquette when it comes to the phone, maybe you shouldn't use it, since apparently you are inconsiderate.

While on the subject of phones, let's talk about, well, you read, I will write about people who use cell phones while driving but can't actually multi-task.

Cell phones

The National Highway Traffic Safety Administration report published by Donna Glassbrenner, PHD on Driver Cell Phone use in 2005. 6% of drivers are talking on a hand-held cell phone at any given time. When hands-free devices are added this number increases to 10%.

I have checked how I drive and I usually drive slightly over the speed limit but the few times I actually used my cell phone while driving I checked my speed and it slowed down to the actual speed limit. While I have found this is not typical of most I have seen some like myself who still drive the speed limit. I have also seen a few who still drive over it though. Next time you're on your cell-phone and driving, check to see how you're driving.

I recently enabled voice dialing and keep a hands free set in my car, which I believed was safe. I knew the smart thing would be to not use my cell phone while driving. I hate talking on the phone so I use it very rarely. In fact I hardly use it when I am not driving. I hate using the phone because I spend 8 hours a day at work talking on one.

I believed using a hands-free device was safer than using the actual cell phone.

I believed most car accidents involving cell phone users happened when they were dialing the number and not just talking.

Strayer, Drews and colleagues in 2001 released a study showing that hands-free cell phones to be just as distracting as handheld cell phones. The 100-car naturalistic study conducted by <u>Virginia Tech Transportation Institute researchers</u> and <u>NHTSA</u> tracked 100 cars and drivers for one year period. The data contains about 2 million vehicle miles, almost 43,000 hours of data. During this study, the report shows 69 Crashes, 731 Near-crashes and 8295 Incidents.

The study shows that wireless devices are the highest contributor involved in secondary distractions. Dialing hand-held phones and talking/listening were the two greatest reasons.

If you think that is bad, read on. This will really blow your mind.

University of Utah psychologist conducted a three-year study, which shows that motorists who talk on handheld or hands-free cellular phones are as impaired as drunk drivers. The study shows using a cell phone while driving is equal to driving with the impairment equivalent to a blood-alcohol of .08%, which is legally drunk.

Compared to undistracted drivers the study found that motorists talking on either handheld or hands-free drove slower. 9% slower to hit the brakes, 24% more variation in following distance and 19% were slower to resume normal speed after applying the brakes.

Drunk drivers with a .08% blood-alcohol drove slower than both drivers using cell phones and drivers who were not distracted, they drove more aggressively, they were twice as likely to break 4 seconds before a collision would have happened and 23% used more force when breaking.

If you look at both studies together it doesn't make sense for a state to pass a law requiring drivers to use hands free devices since it does not change anything.

As I was writing this book, my friend Tarick and I recorded the amount of cell phone users driving on the highway, the sex of the driver and the speed they were driving were the only things we recorded. A majority of the people who were using their cell phones while driving had an average speed below the actual speed limit. Some of these people drove in the slow lane on the highway but that was very few. Most drove in the fast lane or the middle lane.

Speed	*Men*	*Ladies*	*Total*
-1 to -5	49	18	67
-6 to -10	25	21	46
-11 to -20	8	4	12
+1 to +5	11	1	12
+6 to +10	1	3	4
+11 to +20	3	1	4

46.2% of the people were driving one to five miles per hour under the speed limit. 31.7% of the people were driving six to ten miles per hour under the speed limit 8.2% of the people were driving eleven to twenty miles per hour under the speed 8.2% of the people were driving one to five miles per hour over the speed limit. 2.7% of the people were driving six to ten miles per hour over the speed limit. 2.7% of the people were driving eleven or more miles per hour over the speed limit.

During the study

One driver who was on the phone came from the slow lane all the way over to the fast lane without looking, forcing me into the break down lane.

One driver went from doing 80 mph in the fast lane to doing 50 mph when they picked up the cell phone.

I know phones are an important part of our society, but if you cannot drive safely while on the phone then pick driving or talking since you can't do both at the same time. Since we are talking about phones, this is the perfect chance to talk about calling companies.

Calling Companies

In everyday life you need things that require you to call a company. You need to place an order, call for tech support, get answers to your questions or call to complain about poor service. When you call, the person on the phone will usually try to help you the best they can. They may not always have the answer you want, they may have to transfer you to a different department and they cannot change the policies of the company. There are certain things the person will need in order to help you. There are certain questions they may ask you to understand the best way to help you or to find the best service for you. Most people want to get off the phone with a company as soon as possible. If you want to actually make things faster for yourself, you should have the following information ready for the representative. If you do not know this information, find it out before calling the company. If you're not authorized on the account, let the authorized person call. This is not done to cause you an inconvenience but for the security of the account.

They will ask for the full name on the account.

They will ask for the phone number on the account

They will ask for the address on the account

They may need to verify the last 4 numbers of your social security number.

Things the employee doesn't need to know.

Your life history
The entire history of your account

While the person will usually engage in a general conversation with you, some things should remain private. When you call for technical support you should follow some general rules so you don't look like an idiot.

Don't bother telling them what your friend thinks the problem is. If they were right you would not be on the phone with tech support.
Don't tell them you have certifications or are the Network Admin unless you are. If you lie about it, they will know within the first few questions.

When the rep asks you a question, if you don't know the answer, tell them you don't know. When you make up the answer it makes you sound stupid. Don't try to guess what they are going to ask you to do. This will only delay the call and annoy you and them.

Most people will call for technical support for their computers or Internet. So let's cover this subject too. You spend a lot of money for a computer and you should know how to take care of it.

Computers

Computers have become a part of our everyday life. Most households have at least one computer today and while they do make life easier there are certain things that you should know. Computers require basic maintenance and have unneeded software installed. It would be nice if computers came with something explaining how to protect you and your family from the potential threats that are on the Internet. They don't though. The only way to learn what you should do is if you know someone who knows, take a course or read a book. The companies don't tell you what you need to do to help protect your investment. Your car requires maintenance and tunes-ups, well guess what? So does your computer.

Microsoft Windows © comes on most computers you buy today. You should always keep your operating system up to date. Microsoft has made it easy for you to do this. You set your computer to install updates automatically or you can do it yourself.

Personally I tell all my friends who do use this operating system to do it manually, this way you can know when it is being done and you can see what updates are being installed. Running disk clean up is something you should get in the habit of doing regularly. This will help keep your computer free of junk files that are not needed.

Running disk defrag is something that should be done regularly as well. The frequency of running should be based on how often you install, uninstall and update programs. The more frequently you do this, the more frequent you should defrag. You can choose to either buy a 3rd party disk defragmenter or use the one built into Windows.

There is more you should do to protect your computer, but I am not going to cover it since this isn't a how to book. You want one of those? Go buy *Windows for Dummies* or a book like that. Since computers were covered, let's cover the internet since there are things you should know about that.

The Internet

The Internet allows you access to things you may not normally have access to.

Most people use the Internet for enjoyment but there are some who pose a danger. If you do not protect your family and yourself, No one will do it for you. You are the one responsible for this.

If you do not protect your child they could become the victim of a child predator. If you do not properly protect your information you could become a victim of identity theft. If you do not protect your computers you could get Spyware or a virus.

During the years I have worked in technical support I have heard all kinds of excuses from people about why they don't. The most common is "I don't know how." Did you know how to drive a car before you were taught? You are responsible for the computer and the safety of those who use it. When you use the Internet you have to be aware of the possible threats just like you do when you are out in public.

In my opinion the greatest danger found on the Internet is not identity theft or viruses. It is one that can harm your child. Child predators are using the Internet to meet your child. You protect your child from them the best you can, but this is something many parents are not doing when it comes to the Internet.

Child Predators

If you don't protect your children they could become the victim of a child predator. You can hope your child knows this and won't talk to someone they don't know on the Internet but you need to make sure. The best way to protect them is to educate them on the dangers and install programs that will help you protect them. If you do not know about them; take the time to learn. If you are not sure how to learn you are not alone. The good thing is there are plenty of ways to learn. You can learn by doing research using your computer. You did buy it to use it, right? You can go to the store and buy a book. You can also talk to a sales representative who will help you find what you need.

When you do not protect your family and yourself you really have no one else to blame but yourself. You talk to your children about what is and is not safe in the real world. You know children think they know it all and do not always listen to advice or follow the rules. What makes you think they will when they are on the computer?

If you think they are safe just because it is a computer you really need to think again.

1 out of 5 children were solicited for sex on the Internet
25% of children have been exposed to unsolicited pornography on the Internet.
About 25% of children who encountered a sexual approach or solicitation informed an adult.

About 75% of children willingly share personal information while online.

80% of the online predators will target children 14 or older and 20% of the time children 10 to 13 years of age are the targets.

Less than 25% of all households in the U.S actually use filtering or blocking software on their computer.

If you think chat rooms are the only possible threat to you on the Internet, you need to wake up. As the number of social website's increase so are the ways child predators, scammers and spammers have to target you.

Social websites

When you create a profile, you usually put what city you live in, your age and some will ask you for the school you attend or have attended. People will prompt you for friends. While most have good intentions, there are a few who do not. They are the child predators, spammers and scammers.

Social websites can be a lot of fun and very useful. They can help you find a date, make new friends or help you find old friends you lost touch with.

When you do meet someone, take your time to get to know him or her. There are scammers who will try to get you to give them money. They will live in different countries but say they live around you. In the e-mail they will tell you a fake life history wrapped up in a nut shell and then they tell you they want to start a family and settle down. They will also tell you that they think you are the one for them. Think about this for a minute. Do you really think someone who read a few lines about you and saw your picture can possibly know you're the one for them? If you happen to talk to them, they will usually tell you they are stuck in a different country and need money for a plane ticket to get back to the U.S and they will ask you to send them money. If you do, you're a fool. What would you do if some stranger walked up to you on the street and said all this to you? Would you believe them? If not, why on earth would you believe someone in e-mail?

One of the things on the Internet that annoys almost everyone I know and I am pretty sure it annoys you is spam.

Spam

Spam *is unwanted or unsolicited bulk email. Spammer's will also sell your email address to other spammers.*

Most people who have an e-mail address would love to keep it free of spam but believe it or not you usually cause the problem yourself or your friends do.

Spammers will use any means they can to get e-mail addresses. Some of the ways are:

Chain e-mails
Chat rooms
Websites
Newsgroups

They will also buy them from other spammers.

Don't believe everything you read in an email, just because someone you know forwarded it to you. They may have been gullible but that doesn't mean you have to be.

Spammers have many ways to collect e-mail addresses. They will create a chain email or use one that has been going around the

Internet already. When you forward a chain email you actually cause your email address to receive spam and all the people you forward it to. Now all your friends and family know whom to thank. When you get them they are usually not hard to recognize. Chain emails typically have a set layout to them. Before forwarding one to your friends or family one of these, think about it first. Does the e-mail do one or more of the following?

Tell you to act now by forwarding it. Use an authoritative or newspaper-type tone.

Tell you something bad will happen.

Offer you sex, money, good or bad luck.

Invoke feelings of pity or generosity.

Tell you something cool will happen when you forward it.

If you have an email address you have more than likely received one. Once they get your e-mail address it is almost impossible to stop the spam.

A trick I do is I have multiple e-mail addresses setup. One for my friends and family I tell them not to forward me the chain e-mails no matter how much they want to. One for work and one for things I want to sign up for when using the Internet.

This is an actual copy of chain email that has been sent over the Internet for years. While some of the wording varies based on which one you get they are pretty much the same.

(This email was not sent out by Microsoft, AOL or any legitimate source.)

Subject: FW: Microsoft and AOL merger

Date: Fri, 24 Sep 1999

I'm forwarding a forwarded message...read on, it works you may get $$ from Microsoft. Certainly Bill has enough to share-maybe today we'll be blessed financially!

"I am forwarding this because the person who sent it to me is a good friend and does not send me junk. Microsoft and AOL are now the largest Internet Company and in an effort make sure that Internet explorer remains the most widely used program, Microsoft and AOL are running an e-mail beta test. When you forward this e-mail to friends, Microsoft can and will track it (if you are a Microsoft Windows user) for a two week time period. For every person that you forward this e-mail to, Microsoft will pay you $5.00, for every person that you sent it to that forwards it on, Microsoft will pay you $3.00 and for every third person that receives it, you will be paid $1.00. Within two weeks, Microsoft will contact you for your address and then send you a check. I thought this was a scam myself, but two weeks after receiving this e-mail and forwarding it on, Microsoft contacted me for my e-mail and within days, I received a check for $800.00."

There are just a few problems with this email.

Notice how it says "it works you may get $$." Now, if it really works, why wouldn't they say, "You will get money"?

If Microsoft was actually trying to keep Internet Explorer the most widely used program, why would they be tracking e-mails? If your friend, who forwarded it to you, received a check 2 weeks after forwarding it, how did they get the check before they forwarded it to you?

You can also check for grammar and spelling. Real companies will have all emails checked for these since they want to be professional. There are so many things you can do to protect yourself. The biggest one is common sense.

Also be realistic, do you really think a company is going to pay money to people for just forwarding the email? News flash, it will not happen.

Before you forward an email, think about it, do you really think it is going to happen. If you think it will because the email says it will; then I have a bridge in New York I want to sell you.

Another possible threat on the Internet is a computer virus. A computer virus is a program that infects files, copies itself, can spread to other computers when infected files are exchanged. Often infected files come as email attachments, from people you know and they are totally unaware of the email being sent. There are different types of computer viruses that you should protect yourself from. You can get a virus on your computer a few different ways, some of these ways are;

Emails
Websites
File sharing
Internet downloads
System network connections to other
infected computer media, etc.

The best ways to prevent a virus from getting on your computer is knowledge and an anti-virus that is kept up to date. To help protect your computer from viruses you should keep a high-quality anti-virus program installed and keep it up to date.

Scan files using your anti-virus. Tell your friends to inform you before sending an attachment in an email. If you don't update it or scan your files, there is no point in using it. I am only mentioning a few of the ways you can help prevent them. You should educate yourself on the other steps you can take. Another possible threat via the internet is called phishing.

Phishing

Phishing - *the practice of luring unsuspecting Internet users to a fake website by using authentic-looking email with the real organization's logo, in an attempt to steal passwords, financial or personal information, or introduce a virus attack; the creation of a web site replica for fooling unsuspecting Internet users into submitting personal or financial information or passwords.*

These e-mails will often tell you to click on a link and update your information. The website will look almost like the real one if not an exact duplicate of it. The biggest difference will be the website address you're taken to.

If your bank uses the website address www.bank.com and the website that comes up has www.something.com/bank this is not the real site and you should close out of it right away and contact the company that is being impersonated so they can take the steps to have it removed.

There are a few things you can look for in one of these emails that usually give it away.

Poor spelling
Poor grammar
The sending email address
Threaten to close your account unless you act now.

While these are things that can help you identify them do not solely rely on them. If you get an email asking you to update your billing information do not click on the link in the e-mail, contact the company. A majority of companies will never ask you in an email to click on a link and update your information. If your information is out of date, they will usually interrupt your service so you will call them.

If you fall victim to this and did not do anything to verify if the email was legit then you have no one else to blame but yourself. You should know how to protect yourself and your family; it is your responsibility to learn it

Some people still communicate by mail (No, not e-mails, I actually mean mail), but in this day and age you receive more junk mail than probably anything else.

Junk Mail

You receive on average about 41 pounds of junk mail per year. If junk mail could be stopped it would save more than 100 million trees annually. The average person uses 700 pounds of paper products annually. This means about 1/3 of the material in landfills are paper products.

Most junk mail ends up right in the trash, so pretty much it is a waste of a company's money to send it. There is a National Do Not Call Registry, so why isn't there a National Do Not Mail Registry? There actually is one, www.PrivacyCouncil.org or you can call your local post office and request all junk mail stopped being delivered to your address. Stopping junk mail to your house will not only save you time but it will save the environment.

There are many ways you, companies and the Government can help reduce the amount of trash that ends up in a landfill. If mandatory recycling laws were passed for paper, plastic and glass products the amount of space used in landfills could be reduced and valuable resources could be saved.

Recycling one ton (2,000 lbs.) of paper could potentially save:

17 trees
6,953 gallons of water
3 barrels of oil.
587 pounds of air pollution
3.06 cubic yards of landfill space
4,077 Kilowatt-hours of energy

Recycling one ton (2,000 lbs) of plastic bottles could save:

Approximately 3.8 barrels of oil.
Approximately 12,000 BTUs of heat energy.

Recycling one ton (2,000 lbs) of glass could save:

1,300 pounds of sand
410 pounds of soda ash
380 pounds of limestone
160 pounds of feldspar. (GPI.org)

If companies started to find ways to reduce the amount of paper they used annually it would not only benefit the earth it would also benefit them. One way a company could reduce costs would be to reduce the sizes of the boxes they use. How many times have you sent away for something and when you received it, the box is much larger than the actual item you sent away for?

I recently had to replace my cell phone and while I will not mention the company's name, I was told I had to bring my cell phone to the local authorized repair center. When I did, they looked at my phone and determined that I needed a new one. Instead of just replacing the phone I had to wait for a new one to be mailed to my house and then send my old one back. Which I thought was pretty stupid since I was at the store and they had the phones in stock. A few days later I received the package with my cell phone. The box was about 10 times larger than the actual phone. I opened the box and there was plastic bubble wrap, under that was another smaller box which was slightly larger than my cell phone. Had they just replaced my old phone right then and there, it would have saved them the cost of the box used to ship the phone, cost for shipping and handling and the cost of the call into the call center to have the new phone activated. This might not seem like much but if the company looked at it from a cost perspective, they could save money. Let's say the company spends $1.00 for the box,

$.50 for the bubble wrap and $.50 for the additional box which was placed inside in the bigger box. Then let's say it cost those companies $2.00 for shipping and handling each way, the total cost for the company would be $6.00. Now if they do this 1 million times per year, this could save the company 6 million dollars. This does not even include the cost into the call center. Now what company would not love to save 6 million dollars per year?

This is not the first time I have received packages from a company where the box was much larger than the item it contained. While I understand the box should be a little bigger to help protect the item from getting damaged, I have to wonder how many trees could be saved each year if the box was only 5 times larger instead of 10 times larger than the item it contains. While reducing the sizes of the boxes would save trees it would also reduce the cost for the company.

I am not sure who makes some of the policies for some companies but if a company's goal is to make money shouldn't the policies made by the company reflect this? Maybe they should hire me to go in and find ways to cut costs since apparently the people who are making the decisions now are not very good at it.

While on the topic of saving the environment I have to talk about cars.

Cars

In America the average automobile gets 20 miles per gallon (mpg). Federal standards estimate the average person drives 15,000 miles per year. Which means the average person uses 750 gallons of gas annually. The current standard for new passenger automobiles is 27.5 mpg. Which means all new passenger automobiles should use roughly 546 gallon of gas annually. If the average gas mileage requirement were increased to 35 mpg then you would use roughly 429 gallons of gas annually.

I mention all this because over 100 years ago the 1908 Model T had an average of 25 miles per gallon. So if the average was 25 miles over 100 years ago shouldn't you be able to expect more from today's vehicles?

I do realize the cars of today do more than automobiles from the previous years but shouldn't the goal of car companies be to improve all aspects of the car rather than just add more luxuries?

While on the topic of cars, I have to mention the way some people drive.

Driving

I remember when I was a teenager driving around with my friend Andy. We did a lot of driving around. We would go down a road just to find out where it took us. When driving around back then people tended to drive safer. Occasionally an idiot would do something stupid and we would give them the one finger salute. Times have changed since then and so have the driving habits of people.

Some drivers pull out in front of people just because they have their turn signal on even when it is unsafe for them to do so. Just because you have your turn signal on, does not mean you have the right of way or traffic has to yield. Wait until it is safe to pull out. People who are merging onto the highway think the ones on the highway have to stop to let them in. You're merging on to the highway, when you pull on the highway at a much slower rate of speed you can cause an accident or slow down all the other drivers because you could not wait to merge.

People who stay in a lane that is moving faster so they can cut in line at a closer spot, and avoid waiting are just rude. While I have done this a couple of times accidently when I had no idea where I was going, I do try not to. You actually cause more of a delay for everyone else when you do this.

As you drive down the road how many times have you seen people who have broken down?

I remember a time when people actually helped each other when they saw someone broken down on the highway. I actually have a friend who reminded me how nice it feels to help someone. We were driving down a highway and took an exit, at the intersection there was a vehicle broken down blocking traffic, which resulted in the back up of traffic. People kept going around the vehicle instead of helping the lady. My friend Jerry and I stopped to help push the vehicle out of the way which took us about 2 minutes. By doing that one thing we helped clear the vehicle out of the way and helped save time for all the drivers who would be coming up the same way.

I know today, many people tend to be afraid of what could happen if they stopped to help someone on the side of the road, but if you keep thinking like this you are letting the fear run your life. I would not suggest you stop if you feel uncomfortable, but why not at least call for help for the person.

There are three types of people who drive; ones who drive under the speed limit, at the speed limit and over it. Which are you?

I use the highway regularly and so many people use the fast lane that drive under the speed limit. I respect your choice to drive the speed you feel comfortable with, but you should move out of the way for the people who actually want to drive the speed limit. It pisses me off when a driver uses the fast lane and drives slower than the speed limit posted. Have the common courtesy to drive in one of the other lanes instead. If you are not going fast then why are you in the fast lane?

Also, there are people who like to drive faster than the posted speed limit. While I agree that posted speed limits should be followed, let's admit it, not everyone does. I tend to be one of those people at times so when a driver wants to go above the speed limit, let them pass. You're not the police and you are not the one who will get pulled over. Try moving over and think, "Better them than me." How many times have you heard someone say there should be a driving test for people over a certain age?

I have heard so many people say that after a certain age a person should be required to take a driving test every few years. This would be a great idea if it were just old people driving this way. If driving the posted speed limit is not something you can handle then you should take a different route that has posted speed limits you feel comfortable with. Ask someone to drive for you. If these don't make sense to you then at least have the respect to pull over when you get a line of cars behind you. While driving around you probably listen to the radio and inevitably hear commercials.

Advertisements

Companies hire advertisement agencies to help them sell their products all the time, you know this though.

Over the past years you have heard and seen commercials telling you what you can change about yourself. There are products available to you and procedures you can get to change something. In most of the commercials or advertisements they also say how much better you will feel or how you can have more confidence. Has society come to a point that flaws are not acceptable? If you have something wrong with your body you can get plastic surgery. If you have poor eyesight, you can go see the eye doctor and have it corrected it. Most of them will tell you how confident you will be with this change. Do you really think you can get instant confidence this way?

Confidence *is the belief in oneself and one's powers or abilities.*

Do you really think you will be able to do something better just because your appearance changed? If for some reason it does happen to you, how long before the next advertisement tells you something else about you needs to be changed? If you let advertisement agencies and companies tell you how you feel, how will you ever really be happy?

The best way to be happy with you is to be yourself. Screw what others think. The only opinion of you that should matter is yours.

Don't let some advertisement company tell you how to feel about yourself. You can see advertisements whenever you watch TV.

Watching TV

While watching TV there are many shows and channels for you to watch. You can learn all kinds of things when you watch TV. However, there are some things that should not be shown on TV. Here are just three examples of shows that should not be broadcasting but were.

I was flipping through the TV stations and came across a show that revealed how a terrorist could disable America by using an E.M.P (Electro Magnetic Pulse) and it showed the best place to use it. What on earth were they thinking when they did this?

Did they even think maybe a terrorist might be watching TV?

About 3 or so years ago I watched a show that detailed how a person was killed and how no evidence was left. The TV show actually broke it down and even explained why it worked. The killer was never found. Basically for anyone who watched this show, it demonstrated how to commit the perfect murder. What idiot had the bright idea to make this show and who decided to air it? I have to wonder if the thought of teaching someone how to commit the perfect murder was a bad idea.

I enjoy watching martial arts shows very much since I have studied the art. The producers of martial arts shows while very educational; really need to think about what they are doing before they air it. I know how deadly martial arts can be and I also know how serious you can injure someone. When a TV show breaks down the moves and demonstrates how to perform the move they are basically showing people how to execute the move. Without the proper training if someone uses these moves in a fight it can result in serious harm to either the attacker or defender and possibly death.

Martial arts requires the proper training and watching a TV show or learning it from a book is not the proper way to learn it. There is much more to martial arts than just the techniques, which cannot be learned from a book or by watching a 60-minute TV show.

When a TV show is produced no matter how educational it may be, they should stop to think, what if the wrong person watches this show? Putting a warning on the show does not prevent someone from doing it; it just protects the company from potentially being sued. Shouldn't they have the intelligence not air certain types of shows? You may think no for one reason or another but consider this. How would you feel if someone you loved was injured or even killed as a result of something someone else learned from a TV show?

In life so many things have to be politically correct so you don't hurt someone's feelings. Don't expect that in this book. If you want someone to be politically correct read a different book. Remember the warning label? If you don't, here is a reminder.

WARNING:

Some topics contained in this book are not politically correct and may upset you. Read this book at your own risk. The publisher and author may not be held responsible for any emotional, financial or any other type of damages resulting from you reading this book. You bought it.

Not politically correct

Religion

While I believe religion is a personal choice
and one does not have to go to a church to
believe in a higher power, many people may
disagree with me, so be it. Everyone has the
right to believe the way they feel is right for
them.

Just because someone believes differently
then another does not make him or her
wrong or a bad person. Very religious
people have told me on occasion "You're
going to burn in hell." Reality check, this is
judging someone. So you may want to read,
Mathew 7:1 "Don't judge other people, or
you will be judged."

I remember a time in America when the
students would pledge allegiance to the flag
every morning in school. This was stopped
because of the word "God" in the pledge.
Why? Because some people said it was
offense to them.

The definition of God varies by dictionary,
however, they all basically describe the
definition as the Supreme Being; creator of
the universe.

I do not see what the problem is with having children say the pledge of allegiance to the flag for the country they are citizens of. If saying that one word in the pledge is offensive to you then get over it.

I pledge allegiance to the flag of the United States of America and to the republic for which it stands, one nation under God, indivisible with liberty and justice for all.

I realize there are people who may not believe in a higher power. That is fine. But why should an entire country need to change as a result?

The next thing that will happen is saying "God bless you" to someone who sneezes will be offensive. I mean, come on, where will it stop?

While it is nice to show respect to someone for their beliefs why don't they have to show the respect back? Is it really just one sided?

There are things worth fighting for and there are things that are not important enough to fight over.

Politicians

Politicians will always exist as long as there is any type of leadership for a country. However, you should be able to trust and believe in politicians, but do you actually? You should have a reasonable expectation that politicians are obeying the laws and following the Constitution of the United States. Are you surprised when a politician breaks the law, lies and commits adultery?

Do you really believe they are any more honest than anyone else in the country? Most of us know politicians lie. If you don't then where have you been? Why don't they just be honest? They would get more respect that way. If a politician was actually honest how shocked would you be?

Political Lies

Why are you so surprised or angry when a politician lies about something?

On 6 March 03 Hillary Clinton's remarks to a group named CodePink a few weeks before the Iraq War began contradicted all of her claims she made in her first campaign stop in Iowa.

1988 Bush repeated over and over "Read my lips. No new Taxes" but taxes had to be increased to try and reverse the deficit. He was aware taxes had to be increase since Dukakis said taxes had to be increased.

1992 Clinton admitted to smoking pot but stated he did not inhale.

1998 Clinton denies an affair with Monica Lewinsky then changes it to saying they never had sexual relations.

Politicians have been caught cheating on their spouses and lying to us numerous times. If you look at history some have lied because they believe the American people did not want the truth, did not want to hear it or can't deal with it. Some have also lied to get our votes.

Now, how would you act if a politician stood up and actually told the truth instead of a lie? Would you be shocked?

Lie is a type of deception in the form of an untruthful statement with the intention to deceive

Ethics are encompassing right conduct and a good life.

If you get upset now when people lie to you then why do you accept lies from the people who represent us?

If they lie now how can you actually expect them not to lie when making deals on behalf of the United States?

Shouldn't they be held accountable for their actions? Maybe the United States Office of Government Ethics should enforce ethics. You have a right to expect the leaders of your country to be ethical. If most people believe politicians lie then why do you believe them when they make campaign promises?

Campaign promises

Every politician makes campaign promises. How many have actually kept them? While you would appreciate lower taxes, a better economy and more jobs in America a politician can say they will do this but it is not up to just one person.

While the intention is good, I would rather have one of them tell us how they actually plan on doing it instead of just telling us they will. They can all say they will do something but it does not mean they will. I would love it if a presidential hopeful would say. "I will submit legislation to reduce taxes and create new jobs in the U.S" or "I will submit legislation to give incentives to companies who employ American's instead of outsourcing" but over all, it's up to Congress and the Senate to approve the bills.

Scandals

 Politicians are human and will make mistakes and will commit crimes. You can hope they are above committing crimes, but let's be real, they aren't. I can see when they commit a crime why there has to be an investigation but why on earth when they commit adultery is there one? It appears all over the news for days. The US taxpayer spends thousands of dollars on the investigations to find out. What? They did it? The only people this should matter to are the family members.

I do not care if the president sleeps around on his or her spouse. That is their stupidity for cheating on them in the first place. This does not need to make headline news for days and days. Let it be between the family members. It hurts the family enough finding out it happened but having it rubbed in their faces daily makes it even worse. When the average person cheats on their spouse it does not make headline news and the taxpayers do not have to spend the money on an investigation. So why should it be any different with politicians?

While some may say an investigation should be done because it has to do with the character of the politician, how can you actually believe that? Since a majority believe that politicians lie. If you really think they lie, what kind of character can they truly have?

While talking about scandals, I want to talk about something that makes me sick and often makes me wonder, racism.

Racism

Racism is a belief or doctrine that usually involves the idea that one's own race is superior and has the right to rule others.

Many people in life, religious and those who are not religious can be racist. Anyone can be without knowing or realizing it. Sometimes, it is in the words you use or the facial expressions you use when talking to or about someone.

I know racism exists but it has to be one of the stupidest things in society. Hating someone because the color of his or her skin or religion shows how ignorant someone can be. At some time in history almost every race was persecuted.

I will be friends with anyone until they give me a reason not to be. I often wonder how can racism ever be stopped when in certain ways, it is promoted. There is Black history month, a Miss Black America pageant, a United Negro college fund, A Miss Hispanic America pageant and many other things. When the color of someone's skin or race is put into the title of something, isn't that in a way promoting racism? If racism is to truly stop, shouldn't an example be set by not having something for just certain people? While I realize this can be used to promote that races heritage and pride, where is the line drawn? If you heard there was a pageant called "Miss White America" would you consider this to be racial pride or would you think of it as racism?

While talking about racism, there is something I want to mention. While African Americans were slaves in the U.S, almost every race was in slavery at one time or another in history. While no one should ever forget the past, if you did not live through it, how can you be so outraged or upset about it? I hope slavery never happens again on the planet but if everyone bitched about what happened to their race in the past, it would never stop. If you don't think slavery happened to other races, think again and do some research on history.

When one thinks of racism you can't help but to think of the hate groups.

There are hate groups in America who believe in "White Power" and that America should be a white America. News flash for these groups, if you trace your family tree, I am pretty sure you will find out that you came from another country too. While I agree having pride in your nationality or race is important, one race is no better than any other and no nationality is better than any other. As long as you hate someone because of the color of their skin, their belief or where they are from, how can humanity every really grow?

Racism is promoted when a person listens to someone else's belief of racial superiority, yet no race is superior to any other race.

While each race does have idiots in it and
each race has very intelligent people who
strive to make the world a better place.

While change is not easy for most, it takes
time; people have to want the change.

Warning Labels

Most products today come with directions
and warning labels because for some reason,
so many people forgot what common sense
is and have to be told how not to use a
product. When I was younger, if you used a
product wrong and got hurt as a result you
were told, that will teach you. Today though,
so many people want to sue for not being
told how to use or how not to use something.

Whatever happened to common sense and
taking responsibility for your own actions?

Since that seems to be going out the
window. Products have to come with
warning labels letting you know how to not
to use the product.

Warning labels are found on most of the
products sold today. They warn you of
potential harm or how you should not use a
product. Certain products should have
warning labels on them when it is not very
obvious of what could result. Some things
are very obvious and should not have to
have warning labels. Each year lawsuits are
filed and while some are thrown out of
court, others are allowed and monetary

awards are given. Where does a company's reasonability stop and yours start when using products? Has common sense been lost for some people?

How can you not realize when something is hot it can burn you or if a product is flammable it can burst into flames. Should warning labels be put on glass products since they can break and result in you getting cut? If you are going to rely on warning labels to point out the obvious to you, shouldn't people come with them too? People lie, cheat, steal, play head games, are racist and much more. So when someone lies to you and you find out should you sue him or her for the emotional pain? When someone is brutally honest with you and it hurts your feelings, should you sue him or her too?

Life does not come with warning labels letting you know you will experience hurt, sadness, grief or other bad emotions yet you know they happen. Since there are no warnings should you file a lawsuit against your parents for giving birth to you?

If warning labels don't spell out the possible events that could happen if used wrong, who is responsible, you or the company? If companies put a warning label on products spelling out all the potential harm some products would have to come with a book.

When someone gets hurt, there inevitably will be gawkers.

Gawkers

When something tragic happens people tend to stop and watch what is going on. While some people may stop to actually help, how many are just being nosey? When there is a car accident on the north bound side of a highway, why do people on the south bound of the highway feel the need to slow down and look? All this is doing is causing the potential for another accident. Stop being so damn nosey and pay attention to what you are doing.

The greater the amount of people who stop to watch increases the bystander effect. This is a social phenomenon in which the presence of other people reduces helping behavior.

While writing about this topic, I attempted to locate statistics on car accidents resulting from gawkers from the National Highway

Traffic Safety Administration. The NHTSA website did not have statistics for car accidents resulting from onlookers or gawkers that I could find. The email address link on the site was down and the number provided to me for the statistics department was no longer in service.

When something happens to you and you are being assisted, do you really want other people standing around taking pictures or filming the accident? Or would you rather have some kind of privacy?

Privacy

Privacy is the act of secluding oneself.

When you want privacy you hope and
expect others to respect it. Everyone should
be entitled to privacy no matter who they
are. When your privacy is not respected it
can provoke powerful feelings. There are
things in life you wouldn't want others to
know about. Now, shouldn't everyone's
privacy be respected?

If you agree, then ask yourself why someone
who is famous does not deserve this as well?
Shouldn't they be able to determine what
gets published about their private life? Do
you find it acceptable that someone who is
famous has very little privacy? There are
magazines, TV shows, radio shows and
websites dedicated to providing us
information about them. On the survey I did
for this book, I asked the question, "Do you
feel when someone becomes famous they
should lose the right to privacy?" When
people who participated in my survey said
yes I would ask them why. The reason
given was they chose to live in the public
eye. Which is true for the most part, they
did. Even though they chose to work in the

113

public eye, shouldn't they have the same right to privacy as everyone else?

Britney Spears was taken to a hospital by ambulance and it had to be given a police escort because of paparazzi. This resulted in the taxpayers paying around $25,000. Shouldn't the paparazzi have paid for it and not the taxpayers? When paparazzi's crowd around a star to take pictures they do not care what is going on or whom the pictures affect. Shouldn't they be held responsible for their actions?

Now, if someone followed you around every day and took pictures of you doing whatever you were doing, would you mind? Would you call the police and have them arrested for stalking? Now, if this is` stalking, how come paparazzi's do this all the time without getting in trouble? Oh, wait, freedom of the press, right?

"Congress shall make no law respecting an establishment of religion, or prohibiting the free exercise thereof; or abridging the freedom of speech, or of the press; or the right of the people peaceably to assemble, and to petition the government for a redress of grievances."

I believe in the Constitution, but taking pictures of famous people on the beach, eating dinner, shopping or other "normal" activities should not be protected by the Freedom of the Press.

Can you really blame the paparazzi or the tabloids? Yes. But you can also blame the people who buy the magazines and watch the TV shows. Next time you watch the TV shows, buy a tabloid or listen to it on the radio. Ask yourself, how you would feel if it was your family member or yourself they were talking about or pictured. Should they be covered by the freedom of the press or should this be considered stalking?

Stalking: *To follow or observe a person especially out of obsession or derangement. This includes following the person to certain places, to see where they live or what the person does on a daily basis.*

How can what paparazzi's do not be considered stalking?

Things you can change within society

Unemployment

Within society there are many things that should be changed. The best place to start would be the economy. You can easily blame the companies for closing factories in America and moving them overseas. You can blame the U.S. Government for not fixing the loophole in the tax laws. You should also blame yourself for buying foreign made products and not products made in the US. We should actually stop looking for someone to blame and look for ways to fix it.

The economy and unemployment rates get worse each year. While the U.S Government tries to help by sending tax rebates, it does not actually work in the long run. For the U.S. economy to improve one of the best places to start is by creating jobs in America. If people have jobs, they will spend the money. Americans are getting laid off each year and it is getting harder for them to find a job. When someone is out of a job, they have to watch what they spend so they will not buy something unless they actually need it.

A way to create jobs is to give companies a reason to stay in America and not outsource overseas. There is a loophole in the U.S tax laws that allow companies to pay fewer taxes if they outsource to another country instead of keeping the jobs here.

While it is great to try and help other countries with jobs shouldn't the economy in your own country come first? Who can blame the companies for going overseas and not staying here in America? You are just as responsible for companies going overseas as the Government for not fixing this loophole.

Companies are in the business to make money. When the cost of doing business is more expensive in America than for a company to open a factory overseas, why would a company not move overseas?

Companies need to have a reason to make the products in America. If the tariff on imported products is increased and if the taxes on products made in America are decreased, this would give them a reason.

Your responsibility

We all want to buy the merchandise as cheap as possible and get the most for our money. With the current economy it makes perfect sense. However, we fail to see the big picture. If we keep buying products from the companies that import and deal with companies who outsource overseas you are contributing to American jobs being lost. The companies who try to stay in America might be a little more expensive because they have to pay American wages and taxes.

Two companies who make the same product; one is made in America and one based overseas. The American company who pays higher wages and provides benefits charges $50.00 for the product. The company based overseas who pays lower wages and provides no benefits charges $40.00 for the product. Which would you buy? Most people will buy the cheaper priced product. How does this affect the jobs in America? If the American company sells fewer products because of the $10.00 cost difference they have to find a way to compete with the other company. They either have to cut jobs in America by laying some people off or move over seas. Now if people were willing to pay the $10.00 price difference and buy American, then the company would have to make more because of the demand, which would then in turn require them to increase the work force. So how is this not partly your fault?

You really can't blame just the Government or the companies for this. You should be willing to take some of the blame on yourself and admit it.

While writing this book I have found out many people vary on how they feel about this. Most who said it could not be contributed to the American people blamed the Government. I have to wonder, If you can blame the government for it, then aren't you still admitting partial blame for it, since the Government is made of elected officials? If you're not emailing them or calling them to demand things change how is it not partially your fault?

You can also put some of the blame on the people who file all those frivolous lawsuits. The companies have to recover the cost of the lawsuit from someplace. Where do you think this comes from?

Frivolous lawsuits

In today's society you can sue anyone for almost any reason. Over the years I have laughed at some of the lawsuits I have heard about. I have never laughed as hard as when I did a search on the internet for frivolous lawsuits and found the website *legalzoom.*com which contained the top ten. Frivolous lawsuits need to stop. It is not only the person who files the lawsuit who is to blame, but it is the Justice system's fault as well for not throwing it out of court. I will admit there are times when a lawsuit should be filed, but there are times they should not be allowed.

In 1992 McDonald's was sued when a customer spilled hot coffee on her legs and received third degree burns on 6% of her body. McDonald's had to pay $160,000 because she was found to be twenty percent at fault. She was also awarded $2.7 million in punitive damages.

I have worked in two different amusement parks when I was younger and in one, I was a ride operator. Rides have height restrictions for no other reason than safety. When I was working one Friday night a few intoxicated people were in line and one had a baby with them. The height restriction for the ride was 54 inches; the baby was maybe 24 inches. The adult who was holding the baby wanted me to let the baby on the ride and when I refused for safety reasons he offered me $20.00. When I refused again, he offered me $30.00. I refused again and he started yelling and screaming about it.

Now this did not just happen once while I was employed at the amusement park, it happened multiple times a night and while some people were drunk, most were not. Not all offered me money but most used some pretty colorful words. Now had I let any of those people on the ride and something happened to the child they would have sued the park and I would have lost my job.

A Senator filed a lawsuit against GOD. The lawsuit stated: "God has made and continues to make terrorist threats of grave harm to innumerable persons." It states the threats were credible, given God's history. It also stated God and his followers caused "widespread death, destruction and terrorization of millions upon millions of the Earth's inhabitants," as well as "fearsome floods, egregious earthquakes, horrendous hurricanes, terrifying tornadoes, pestilential plagues, ferocious famines, devastating droughts, genocidal wars, birth defects, and the like." The suit asked the court for a summary judgment or for an injunction against God from engaging in the acts detailed in the suit. This lawsuit was filed in protest of frivolous lawsuits. They were trying to show that in this country, you can sue anyone for any reason. The senator was trying to get a bill passed to limit frivolous lawsuits.

When a person is injured on private property while in the process of committing a crime, they should not be allowed to sue the owner of the property.

Some lawsuits are just freaking stupid and should not be allowed. When lawsuits are filed that are frivolous should the lawyers who accept the cases be blamed, the judges who do not throw the lawsuit out of court or the people who want them filed? You should blame them all. The people who filed them for not taking responsibility, the lawyers and judges who allow them for not having enough common sense to say, "No, you can't do this.

My thoughts

The Police

It takes a special kind of person to be a
police officer; they protect and help us in
our time of need. They answer our calls for
help when other people will just pass by or
act like they do not hear our cries for help.

They can't be doing it for the pay since the
starting pay for a police officer is about
$51,000 a year as of May 2008. They can't
be doing it for the appreciation because the
only time they are appreciated is when you
need them. Other than that do you really
want them around?

Why do men and woman decide to become a
police officer? They know how little they
get paid and they are aware of how little
respect they are shown. I honestly believe
they do this because they want to help
people.

While some people think they do it for the
power trip or because they get off arresting
people, they do not make the laws of society
they only enforce them.

They do not go around looking for people to
arrest. They arrest a person when a crime is
committed. When they do arrest a person

for a crime, the person almost always denies it.

When you get pulled over for speeding do you act like you were not speeding and think the police officer is wrong for pulling you over?

I cannot even begin to image how many times a police officer has heard someone deny speeding, a traffic violation or committing a crime, even when they know they did it.

I was pulled over a few months back on my way to work. I was not paying attention to my speed at all but I knew I was speeding. I was pulled over and when the police officer asked me if I knew why he was pulling me over, I told him the truth. I was speeding. He asked me if I knew how fast I was going. I told him I honestly have no clue. He was surprised because I was honest about it and I did not deny it. I told him I was not going to lie to him about it and he told me I would be surprised how many people do. When you break the law and lie about it you are basically telling the police officer he is stupid. Why not just admit what you did and accept responsibility for it. Try a little honesty with a police officer; it does go a long way. If you think that is too difficult then think about it this way: How do you feel when someone lies or acts like you're stupid?

Next time you get pulled over or deal with police think about how you want them to treat you. If you don't mind being treated like you're stupid then go for it, but if you think the officer is going to give you a break think again. They are actually pulling you over or talking to you because they have a reason.

The police deal with all kinds of people during their career. They will more than likely come across someone carrying a firearm.

Guns

There is a major problem when someone can buy a gun on the streets easier than buying drugs or when the bad guys out gun the good guys. Something needs to change.

While you have the constitutional right to bear arms, there are times when the general public does not need access to certain types of guns.

Permits to own a gun are required and there are gun safety classes in all states, however this does nothing to stop the flow of guns on the streets. As a society more needs to be done to stop gun violence. But as soon as the government tries to pass a law people complain about how they have the right to bear arms.

Do hunters really need a semi-automatic gun? Hunting is a sport and I know people hunt and that is their right. If you have to use a semi-automatic gun to kill the animal you shouldn't be hunting. If you think hunting is a sport, then give the animal a chance to win. Hunt with a bow or a single shot riffle. If you miss, then you lost and the animal won.

You hear about kids going to school and shooting people. This is something that can be prevented if people actually woke up and paid attention. When our children do this, the blame is put on the schools for not noticing that the child was troubled.

Teachers deal with so many children per day, yet they are expected to notice when your child is troubled. Why aren't the parents blamed for not noticing? Shouldn't they have noticed their own child was troubled? You should not be looking to see who is to blame but how it could be prevented in the future.

When violence is committed with guns they will end up in the prison system if not dead. So let's go with the person ending up in prison.

The Prison System

In the prison when a person is incarcerated for a crime, they have access to free cable TV, they can earn a college degree, have access to weights to work out with and full medical. This is more than what some people have who have never committed a crime. How can someone who is sentenced to a prison term get more than someone who works every day?

Insurance

All prisoners get free medical treatment. In 2006, 47 million Americans had no health insurance. Scary, isn't it? Shouldn't the people who obey the laws also get insurance?

College Degrees

There is something wrong when a person
who is incarcerated for a crime can get a
college degree for free and a citizen who has
never committed a crime cannot because of
the cost. Should a prisoner be able to get a
college education at the taxpayers' expense
while someone who has never committed a
crime cannot? Some will disagree with me
because they feel prisoners should be given
an education to help keep them from going
back into prison. Most places that hire
people with degrees also want experience.
If we are not going to give them the
experience in the field, then what is the
point of allowing them to get a free degree?

Shouldn't they be taught a career they can
use when they get out of prison? If they are
taught a vocational skill there is a better
chance of them finding a job when they get
released. Also, the Government could give
the companies who higher them a small tax
break to help increase the chances of them
finding a job that will pay enough so they
will be able to earn a living without
resorting back to a life of crime.

Weights

While I agree giving the prisoners
something to do while they are serving time
this idea is not the greatest. I understand
that prison life is not easy and they need
things to do but should we allow violent
criminals access to weights, which only
makes them stronger. Allowing them to
become stronger seems like a bad idea since
it would allow them to commit violent
crimes easier. Shouldn't we find other
activities for them to do besides allow them
to get stronger?

Prisoner rights

One thing that has bothered me is how
criminals seem to have more rights than the
victims. How many criminals have stopped
and thought "I can't violate this persons
civil rights?" yet the criminals rights are
always protected and they get a free
education, medical insurance, free room and
board and who knows what else. While I
know their freedom has been taken away
from them and I would image prison life is
not easy, they still get more then some of the
victims get.

Some people are in prison for violent crimes and there are some who are incarcerated for non-violent crimes. There are inmates who are incarcerated for the charge of possession of marijuana only. Not with intent to distribute or trafficking, just for personal use.

Marijuana

In the US the FBI estimates about 40% of Americans ages 12 and older have smoked marijuana at least once.

In 2006, according to FBI statistics 738,915 Americans were arrested and charged with marijuana possession only.

Department of Justice reports show that 12.7 percent of state inmates and 12.4 percent of federal inmates incarcerated for drug violations are serving time for possession of marijuana only and no other charges. This does not show how many were repeat offenders.

In December of 2006, there were 2,258,983 prisoners in federal and state prisons. If you take the average of the two, it means 282,372 inmates were incarcerated for possession of marijuana only.

The average annual cost per incarcerated inmate in 2008 to the taxpayers is roughly $35,000. The total cost for the taxpayers annually comes out to $9,883,020,000

Putting people on probation or house arrest instead of in prison for the sole charge of possession of marijuana and putting those in prison on one or the other would save the taxpayers' money due to these reduced costs. It would also save the taxpayers' money in other ways.

When a person is incarcerated and they are a parent, the result is the loss of income to the house, which makes the other family members suffer. Now if they were the only income in the household the spouse then has to go on public assistance which means you are not only supporting the one who committed the crime but their family as well.

The government declared war on drugs and spends billions of dollars on it each year. Yet it is a war that will never be won. As long as people want it, they will find a way to get it. Declaring war on a drug that is actually proven to have medical benefits seems stupid to me. The tax dollars could be used in other areas, which would actually benefit people. The government could tax it just like cigarettes and use the money generated in more beneficial areas.

The estimated cost to taxpayers in the U.S for the war on marijuana is over 42 billion dollars per year.

State and local justice costs for marijuana arrests are now estimated to be $7.6 billion, approximately $10,400 per arrest. Of this total:

Annual police costs are $3.7 billion

Judicial/legal costs are $853 million

Correctional costs are $3.1 billion

It is estimated the total value of the marijuana crop in the U.S. is over 35.8 billion dollars.

There has been no death solely contributed to smoking marijuana. Marijuana medically helps nausea, glaucoma, pain and much more. There are stronger medications than marijuana that are legal, which are abused yet they are not made illegal.

Drug treatment

Instead of putting them in prison they could be put in a drug treatment program. One company called _South Coast Recovery_ is only $11,800 (at the time this subject was researched). This means for the amount paid per person to be incarcerated for possession of marijuana, 3 people could get drug treatment. This makes more sense.

Probation

The average cost per person on supervised probation is less than $5,000 annually.

Now, since the person is on probation they can remain working and they could actually pay for 50% of the cost per year saving taxpayers even more money.

House arrest

The average cost per person to be on house arrest is less than $5,000 annually.

With the person on house arrest, they could be allowed to leave the house to go to work only. This would allow them to be charged 50% of the cost (depending on the person's income).

Another pointless thing is to arrest and put people in jail for prostitution. I am not saying it is morally right or wrong, that is up to them. I am not them and I am not going to pass judgment.

Prostitution

One of the oldest professions in the world is prostitution. While a few states have made it legal, most have not. Why is it illegal? I visited a few websites and some of them provide reasons why it should remain illegal.

While I agree legalizing it could bring all kinds of other concerns to light and I have checked the statistic's on the people who become prostitutes. Some of the arguments against it are:

Legalization of prostitution is a gift to the pimps.

Actually in a way it could be seen as both but if you look at it this way there are benefits for the prostitute as well. If the pimp beats the crap out of them right now, they cannot call the police for fear of being arrested themselves, but if it was legal then they could call the police without fear of being arrested. Also, if a "john" beats them up, with prostitution legal, they would then be able to call for help without fear of being arrested.

Legalization of prostitution promotes sex trafficking.

Sex trafficking is happening all over the world now, so how does making prostitution legal promote sex trafficking? That is just a stupid thought.

Legalization of prostitution does not give control over the sex industry.

There is no control over it now. At least if it was legal brothels could be setup, giving the person a safer place to do it. Laws could also be enacted requiring them to submit to Sexually Transmitted Disease tests weekly.

Some will argue legalization of prostitution increases child prostitution. Children prostitute themselves on the street as it is, this will not change. The law could require the minimum age of 18 years of age to be a prostitute.

People will continue using prostitutes if it is legal or not. This will not change and prostitutes will continue what they do.

If the average prostitute makes $300.00 per night and works 5 nights a week, she makes $1500.00 a week; this means she earns $78,000 a year. Now if it was made legal and there are, let's say, 1 million prostitutes in America, this means $78,000,000,000 goes untaxed per year.

While this may not be the safest profession, I believe legalizing it would save the tax payers money.

Why is prostitution illegal anyways? It is not violating anyone's constitutional rights or violating someone's civil liberties.

When a prostitute gets arrested, she is put into the overcrowded prison system.

Overcrowding

Millions of dollars are spent on enforcement, court fees and prison.

America locks up more people than any other country which is resulting in overcrowding in the US prison system.

There is a major problem with the US prisons, overcrowding. If alternative ways of punishment are put into effect for certain crimes this would reduce the prison population making room for more violent criminals.

Another problem with the US prison system is criminals go in and learn how to become better criminals or end up joining a gang for protection. If we offered more effective ways of punishing the nonviolent offenders then hopefully it would reduce the repeat offenders. No matter what types of rules are put into effect in a prison system the criminals will find a way around them.

If we release the prisoners that are incarcerated for non-violent crimes on house arrest or probation, it would reduced the prison population and save the taxpayers' money.

While putting criminals in prison is a good thing, there are just some things people should not be put into prison for. If they were put on probation or house arrest, they would be able to keep their jobs. They could pay for half the cost for either punishment.

These two steps could potentially save tax payers millions of dollars per year.

This would also reduce the possibility that nonviolent criminals would join a gang for protection; learn how to become a better criminal or both. While this is not a fix all, it is just an idea to help reduce repeat offenders and save taxpayers money.

Smokers & Companies

I know smoking is bad for you and I am fully aware of all the proof out there. Laws keep getting passed which make smoking in public places illegal. While I believe in some places smoking shouldn't be allowed and the rights of the non-smoker should be respected but the rights of the smokers should be as well.

Smokers should have the right to smoke outside. Now, if a smoker walks up to a non-smoker, then the smoker should ask if they mind, but when a non-smoker walks up to someone who is smoking already and complains about it, this is just wrong. You saw them smoking so if you do not like it don't walk up to them. If you decided to walk up to them, then deal with it.

I admit there are times a person has no choice, like in restaurants with both smoking and non-smoking sections which are separated by a little piece of glass. What the hell are they thinking? Do they really believe the smoke will not go into the non-smoking section?

While talking about smoking, I have to talk about the companies who have fired and refused employment to people who smoke. Why do they do this? They do this because it drives up the insurance cost for that company.

A few companies are trying to fire employees for smoking when not at work. There are a number of companies who have already started doing this. This is actually pretty scary that companies are doing this if you look at the much bigger picture. The next page contains three examples of companies without the names but how can you not be outraged about this? Even if you're not a smoker you should be upset about this.

A company based in Michigan banned employees from smoking on their own time in 2007. Employees must submit to random tests that detect if someone has smoked. They must also agree to searches if they are suspected of smoking. Those who smoke can be fired or suspended.

A company in Seattle will not hire anyone who smokes. Employees who smoked before the ban was passed over two years ago are not fired. The down side is they can't get medical insurance through the company.

An airline has a no-smoking policy for employees and new employees must submit to a urine test to prove it.

Such bans are not legal everywhere: More than 20 states have passed laws that bar companies from discriminating against workers for lifestyle decisions.

Now if you compare smoking to skin cancer:

In 2007 skin cancer, directly contributed to the sun, affects one million people each year in the U.S.

Squamous cell carcinoma is the second most common form of skin cancer with more than 250,000 cases diagnosed each year.

Out of the 220,830 new lung cancer cases:

Current smokers: 35-40% of new lung cancer cases.
Former smokers: 50% of new lung cancer cases.

*Never smoked: 10-15% of new lung cancer
cases.*

Skin cancer is the most common of all
cancers. It accounts for nearly half of all
cancers in the United States. More than 1
million cases of non-melanoma skin cancer
are found in this country each year.
Melanoma, the most serious type of skin
cancer, will account for about 59,940 cases
of skin cancer in 2007.

In 2007, an estimated 220,830 new cases of
lung cancer occurred in the U.S.

The sun kills 60,000 people annually;
48,000 from malignant melanomas; 12,000
from other kinds of skin cancer.

Does this mean a person should be fired for
spending too much time in the sun?

If you think it is acceptable for a company to
fire a smoker because it increases the cost of
the medical insurance then what is going to
happen when they start firing people for
issues known to cause other health issues?
Such as:

Obesity

Drink alcohol

Participate in risky activities.

If you think those are unacceptable then why is firing a smoker acceptable? Don't you think companies will fire for other things eventually?

Legal experts fear companies will try to control other aspects of employees' off-duty lifestyle, a trend that is already happening. Some companies are firing, suspending or charging higher insurance premiums to workers who are overweight, have high cholesterol or participate in risky activities.

Don't get me wrong, I know smoking is bad for your health, but if this is allowed what will be next?

Still think it should be ok? Do you drink alcohol? Do you think a company should be able to fire employees who drink?

Alcohol

When I did my survey all the people who said a company should be able to fire a smoker or not hire one gave the reasons "it drives up the cost of insurance" and "smoking is a choice". Well, drinking is a choice and here are some statistics for you. I do drink but I don't drink much. I am not trying to get alcohol banned; I am using it to prove a point.

The next few pages list alcohol statistics. From the National Highway Traffic Safety Administration (NHTSA) 2006 and Center for Disease Control (CDC)

Alcohol statistics show:

More than 100,000 U.S. deaths are caused by excessive alcohol consumption each year

Nearly 14 million Americans meet diagnostic criteria for alcohol use disorders

Youth who drink alcohol are 50 times more likely to use cocaine than those who never drink alcohol.

Across people of all ages, males are four times as likely as females to be heavy drinkers.

More than 18% of Americans experience alcohol abuse or alcohol dependence at some time in their lives.

About 45% of all fatal crashes are alcohol-related for person between the ages of 6-33

Alcohol is the most commonly used drug among young people.

Problem drinkers average four times as many days in the hospital as nondrinkers

Alcohol kills 6½ times more youth than all other illicit drugs combined.

The CDC published a study estimating over 34,000 people died from cirrhosis of the liver, cancer and other diseases linked to drinking to much beer, wine and spirits.

More than half of the 414-child passenger's ages 14 and younger that died in alcohol-related crashes during 2005 were riding with a driver who had been drinking.

Each year, alcohol-related crashes in the United States cost about $51 billion.

Of the 1,946 traffic fatalities among children ages 0 to 14 years in 2005, 21% involved alcohol.

Alcohol-related motor vehicle crashes kill someone every 31 minutes and causes nonfatal injuries to someone every two minutes.

Research shows that alcohol is involved in between 40-70% of domestic violence.

If companies are allowed to fire smokers, then why not allow them to fire people who drink alcohol too. While you may think it is not the same thing, look at the statistics and ask yourself, why wouldn't they?

Alcohol is attributed to the follow:

5% of all deaths from diseases of the circulatory system
15% of all deaths from diseases of the respiratory system
30% of all deaths from accidents caused by fire and flames
30% of all accidental drowning
30% of all suicides
40% of all deaths due to accidental falls
45% of all deaths in automobile accidents
60% of all homicides

Do you still think it is okay for a smoker to be fired or not hired? You must work for an insurance company or hold a managerial position for a company. If not then you better hope you are in perfect health if you have a job. If companies are permitted to legally fire someone just for smoking, what makes you think they will stop there? How do you know they will not look into other things such as obesity, diabetes, depression or one of the many other things that cost them money each year?

You may not agree with smoking but this is a form of discrimination. It could also be just a start. How do you know your company won't find something that does affect you in some way and start firing people for that?

Sexual Offenders

While this is something that would be nice if it did not exist in society, it does exist. When someone is convicted of this they are put onto a website for all to see. If used right this could be a great thing, but there are some things that are not taken into account. If a website is going to continue to list offenders then there are some changes that should be made.

First: The types of offenses that are listed should be explained on the website. Helping viewers fully understand the type of offenses.

Second: Offenses should not be grouped.

Right now, people that take a pee in public can be arrested and are listed on the website if found guilty.

Going to the bathroom in public is something you do not want someone seeing you do nor do you want to see others doing it however this is not something that should get someone listed on the sex offenders website.

I know there was a politician in Michigan who was arrested for going to the bathroom in public but all charges were dropped. Had this been a normal every day person would the charges have been dropped?

I also know there are people on the website that slept with the person they love and married. There is one living in Texas who was 18 years old, when he slept with his 16 year old girlfriend. The mother of the girl found out and did nothing until one day she got upset with the boy. She filed a police report and the police arrested the boy. She later tried to drop the charges but the state had taken over.

This couple is married and has a child together. What makes this really sad is that he still has to register every year as a sex offender.

While I do agree sexual predators should register and people have the right to know when one lives in their neighborhood, I do feel that it should be a case by case basis.

At the time of the research for this subject one state is currently trying to enact a bill where all people in that state found guilty of sexual crimes will be required to have something on their state ID letting people know. This is so stupid because it will cause undo prejudice for the people who are not really sexual predators. I would rather see a tracking system where the police can locate people found guilty of this crime using GPS. This way, the ones who do not register as required can easily be found.

Foster Homes

This topic has a lot of meaning to me. I was a foster child in Massachusetts for many years.

On September 30, 2006 there were 510,000 children in the U.S living in foster homes.

The number of foster children age 10 and under: 270,080

The number of foster children age 20 to 11: 239,924

When I was younger, I came home one day and this lady was at my house. I was told to go pack a few things because I would be going away for a few days. I was not told I would never be returning home, see my friends again or that I should take everything I wanted. While the Social worker was really nice to me, I wished they had told me.

I lived in foster homes for many years and I was even put into a residential program in Lancaster, MA. The only foster home I was ever in that I actually believed cared about me was a temp foster home in Quincy, MA across from an IHOP. I had some that were decent but I had some that I know were pretty bad.

One Christmas I was made to sit in a chair and watch the entire foster family open their Christmas presents.

In a few of the homes, I had one set of clothing I could only wear when the Social worker was coming and the rest of the time, the pants I was made to wear were floods and had rips in them and the shirts were all old, faded and ripped.

One foster home hit me across the face with a belt and I still have the scar on my cheek.

I am not saying all foster parents are bad people, I would imagine most actually care about the child. I have spoken to other foster children who in my eyes were lucky to be placed in homes that cared. You may be wondering why did I not let my social worker's know, I did. Some cared enough to believe me and others didn't seem to care at all.

Now before I turned 18 my social worker gave me the choice to sign myself over to the state until I was 21 or leave foster care.

Did they really think I wanted to stay in the system?

When a child in foster care hits 18, they leave the system and have no help, which I was not aware of. I figured the state would help me out. How do I know this? I left foster care when I was 18 and was on my own. I received no help from the state but to me, that was life.

I was on my own but now I wonder why I did not get help and how many other foster children have had to deal with this as well. When a child is taken from their home to help or protect them, shouldn't this help continue instead of stop?

While most children who are placed in foster homes get families that actually care about them, some don't care about the child. I know one of my foster homes took as many foster children as they could for the money the state pays them per child. I was taken out of that home 2 months later.

The money does help to raise the child when the foster parents actually care about the child. The ones who do it for any other reason should be banned from taking a foster child ever again.

When you take in a foster child for the wrong reasons this can affect the child even more because the child will realize you don't really care about them. How is this actually helping the child?

As an abused child who spent years in foster care I was stereotyped by many people.

Stereotyping

In life, people tend to stereotype other people. There are people who say:

"Abused children become abusers"

"Children from broken homes tend to become trouble makers".

There are many other ways of stereo-typing. Is this right? No. While the child may have a greater chance than a child who had a so called "normal" life, it does not mean they will. Until a child demonstrates a certain type of behavior shouldn't they be given the benefit of the doubt? While it may be good to keep an eye on them, they should not be treated like they will do it.

When does stereo-typing actually start to affect the child's behavior?

If you think it doesn't, you may want to think again because you must truly be a dumbass. How can you really think that stereotyping doesn't affect someone's behavior? As a child if you were told constantly that you are stupid, dumb or lazy in time there is a really good chance you will start to believe it. Once you believe it, you have lost and your chances of overcoming it have greatly decreased. Now if you were told how smart, intelligent, beautiful or handsome you are, would you grow up believing this? You may say no and that may be true but you are probably the type of person who would not be stereo-typed in a negative way and are fortunate. Not all of us have been so lucky.

As a result of stereo-typing a person can be labeled in many different ways, one of the ways is violent.

Violence

Today's generation seems to have become more accepting of violence than what was acceptable many years ago. We can see a change in how acceptable it has become in society by the movies, tv shows and video games that are created today. While these things shouldn't affect how people act, I believe in a small way, they do. They seem to desensitize us.

The more accepting of violence we become as a society, the more prone our children will be to commit violent acts.

It seems all a movie, tv show or video game maker has to do to make it acceptable is put a warning label on it and no one seems to mind.

It seems as time passes by, violence is becoming more socially acceptable.

My girlfriend and I recently went to see a movie that was released in Dec 09 and this was one of the bloodiest movies I have ever seen. Trust me, I have seen plenty of them and none compared to this movie. The reason this made the book was because there were children under the age of ten watching this movie. Granted the movie was good, but it was totally unacceptable for children. This movie was rated R. I always believed rated R movies to mean, No one under the age of 17 admitted. However, I was wrong.

An R-rated motion picture, in the view of the Rating Board, contains some adult material. An R-rated motion picture may include adult themes, adult activity, hard language, intense or persistent violence, sexually-oriented nudity, drug abuse or other elements, so that parents are counseled to take this rating very seriously. Children under 17 are not allowed to attend R-rated motion pictures unaccompanied by a parent or adult guardian. Parents are strongly urged to find out more about R-rated motion pictures in determining their suitability for their children. Generally, it is not appropriate for parents to bring their young children with them to R-rated motion pictures.

After the movies, you can stop by a fast food place and get something to eat unless you filled up on junk food at the theater.

Fast Food

Before I go into this part, let me explain that I worked in the fast food industry for years as an employee and a corporate manager. I know what it is like and what is expected of the employee.

One thing that has increased over the years is employees interrupting customers while they order. This shit is just rude and pisses many people off. How many times have you gone through the drive-thru, placed your order and the employee asks; "Would you like cheese on that" or "Would you like the value meal" while you're ordering. I know the employee is just trying to do their job but wait until the person finishes the sentence before you ask.

There is a fast food place right up the street from my house. I use to frequent this place but have since stopped because the employees consistently interrupt me when I place my order. They also messed up my order almost every time I ordered. Typically they would make it wrong 4 out of 5 times. The last time I went the manager was making my food and it took 3 tries to get it right. There was no apology for the long wait or the mess ups. That was the last time I went to this restaurant.

I always believed following directions is not a difficult task, I was actually wrong.

Following directions

Over the years I have noticed that people don't follow directions as well as they use to. I have always wondered how hard it is for people to follow directions. You are given directions almost daily in some part of your life. They are typically verbal or written. I have never found it hard to follow directions but when I did not understand, I have no problem asking questions.

Companies have many policies they want their employees to follow. What good are those policies when the employees do not follow them?

While I am very thankful to all who participated in the survey, it was also another part of the book. All the questions were written certain ways for a reason. This was done to actually find out how many people would follow the directions given to them. While I realize some people may have forgotten them since they may not have done the survey right away. I was surprised to see how many people did not follow directions.

Prior to taking the survey, all people were given the same directions.

- *Answer only yes or no and do not explain any of your answers.*

- *If you think the answer is a maybe, then you should answer yes.*

- *Do not explain any of your answers*

59 out of 86 people followed directions on the first survey.

19 out of 25 people followed directions on the second survey.

Communication is a very important part of giving directions. When someone cannot read them or understand them, it makes it very difficult for them to follow the directions properly.

Language

This topic will probably piss off various people but oh well. Someone has to say it. Why is it that in America there is no national language? The primary language is English but it is not the official language of the country.

It is sad that an entire country has to learn other languages to be able to speak to people. Companies have to put directions in multiple languages and have reps that speak multiple languages. All of this adds additional costs to the products and the consumers have to pick up the tab for it.

How many times have you called a company and heard: "Press 1 for English, Press 2 for Spanish etc…" I know America is "the melting pot" and that she welcomes all people but why should the many accommodate the few? When someone goes to a foreign country, no matter what country it is, they should have to learn the language of that country.

While on this topic, let's talk about how people are trashing the English language everyday with spelling. The word "what" is being spelled "wat", the word "there" is being spelled "ther", the word "right" is being spelled "rite". The work "you" is being spelled "yew". The word "know" is being spelled "noe" and "to" is being spelled "tuh". There are many other words being spelt incorrectly by children.

I remember when I was a child if I spelled a word wrong, I was told the correct way to spell it. Now we have children spelling words wrong on purpose and not being corrected. While the children may think this is cool, as they get older it can become the normal way for them to spell.

It may be the result of text messaging but should this even be acceptable? While there may be a limit on how many characters a cell phone provider allows when you send your text message, proper spelling should still be a priority.

It shouldn't matter what you're writing, proper spelling should always be reinforced.

What can you do?

There are many things you can do to help change things. It all starts with you. If you don't decide to change things with yourself first then trying to change the things within society will be even harder

If you think things need to change, contact your Congressman and Senator and tell them enough is enough or however you want to put it. If enough people in the country do this, then we can all help things change. If they don't want to do what we want, tell them they are not getting your vote when it comes time for re-election. They are all elected officials and the Government is For the People and By the People. When they take office they swear an oath:

"I do solemnly swear (or affirm) that I will support and defend the Constitution of the United States against all enemies, foreign and domestic; that I will bear true faith and allegiance to the same; that I take this obligation freely, without any mental reservation or purpose of evasion; and that I will well and faithfully discharge the duties of the office on which I am about to enter. So help me God."

Contact your Congressman:

www.house.gov

Contact your Senator:

www.senate.gov

If you agree with any part of this book and realize things have to change, then do something about it. Don't hope someone else will do something about it. Do you really think you might be the only one thinking someone else will do it?

The Surveys

Surveys

I conducted two surveys' in which I asked
questions about the topics in this book and
asked those people to answer Yes or No
only and not to explain any of the answers
they provided.

Age, race, nationality or sex where not
considered during the surveys.

Answers that had both yes and no circled
were considered to be yes.

Answers where people wrote in "maybe"
were considered to be yes.

Any answer left bank had the total number
of people questions reduced by one.

1st *survey*

Is there a difference between disciplining a child and abuse?

87 out of 87 people said yes

Should smacking your child on the butt be considered child abuse?

79 out of 87 people said yes

Do you feel telling a child to take a time-out actually works?

57 out of 87 people said yes

Do you feel the lack of discipline is contributing to the violence?

75 out of 87 people said yes

Do you feel children of today have poor manners?

75 out of 87 people said yes

Do you think the prison system in America is currently working as it should?

5 out of 87 people said yes

Do you think prisoners should be allowed to earn a college degree while serving time?

44 out of 87 people said yes

Do you think violent criminals should be allowed to use weights while in prison?

24 out of 87 people said yes

Do you think marijuana should be illegal?

28 out of 87 people said yes

Do you think those in prisons for possession of marijuana only should be put on probation instead? (Personal use)

67 out of 87 people said yes

Do you feel society has become superficial as a result of commercials and advertisements?

74 out of 87 people said yes

Do you feel when someone becomes famous they should lose the right to privacy?

7 out of 87 people said yes

Do you think people concentrate less on tasks when they use their cell phone?

78 out of 87 people said yes

Do you think the economy and unemployment rate can be partly contributed to the American people?

61 out of 87 people said yes

Do you believe politicians lie?

86 out of 87 people said yes

Do you believe tax money should be spent on investigations when a politician commits adultery?

5 out of 87 people said yes

Do you think companies have the right to fire employees for smoking cigarettes off company time?

6 out of 87 people said yes

Do you think a company has the right to refuse employment to a cigarette smoker?

12 out of 87 people said yes

Do you think a company should be able to refuse employment to someone who spends time in the sun?

3 out of 87 people said yes

Do you think using the color of someone's skin or nationality in the name can be considered racism?

44 out of 87 people said yes

Do you think there should be laws limiting the types of lawsuits that can be filed?

63 out of 87 people said yes

Do you think gun laws should be stricter?

23 out of 87 people said yes

2nd *survey*

Should a company have the right to fire an employee who drinks alcohol?

8 out of 27 people said yes.

Should a company have the right to refuse employment to someone who drinks alcohol?

6 out of 27 people said yes

Do you feel cyber-sex is actually cheating on someone?

23 out of 27 people said yes

Do you feel police are under-paid?

16 out of 26 people said yes. (1 person left answer blank)

Do you feel teachers are under-paid?

26 out of 26 people said yes

Do you feel prostitution should be legal if regulated?

15 out of 26 people said yes (1 person left answer bank)

Should politicians be held accountable for campaign promises?

24 out of 27 people said yes

Do you feel a child who commits a crime should not be punished due to age?

9 out of 27 people said yes

Do you think the Government should do more to save the environment?

23 out of 27 people said yes

Do you feel the Government should take Global warming seriously?

24 out of 27 people said yes

Driving study

Age, race or nationalities were not considered during the study.

Michigan highways were used for this study

I-94

I-96

75

Cell phone users were not counted during the following.

During stop and go traffic

Constructions zones

Speeds reduced due to weather conditions

People using hands-free devices

Resources

Definitions have been used with the written permission from Merriam-Webster's Collegiate® Dictionary, Eleventh Edition ©2008 by Merriam-Webster, Incorporated (www.Merriam-Webster.com).

USDOJ - Information generated by the Department of Justice is in the public domain and may be reproduced, published or otherwise used without the Department's permission. Citation to the Department of Justice as the source of the information is appreciated, as appropriate.

NHTSA - Information presented on this web site is considered public information and may be distributed or copied. However, all information submitted to NHTSA/DOT via this site shall be deemed and remain the property of NHTSA/DOT, except those submissions made under separate legal contract. NHTSA/DOT shall be free to use, for any purpose, any ideas, concepts, or techniques contained in information provided to NHTSA/DOT through this site.

FBI Uniform Crime Reports of 2003 and 2006

Preliminary FY 2006 Estimates as of January 2008

The 100-car naturalistic study conducted by Virginia Tech Transportation Institute researchers and NHTSA

Bureau of Labor Statistics

Office of Management and Budget

Paperwork Reduction Act

Center for Disease Control (CDC)

Made in the USA
Charleston, SC
26 April 2010